BABIES BY THE LITTER

Other books by Cheri Gillard

THE RAID OF BALVENIE
AND THE MAIDEN WHO SURVIVED

CHLOE'S GUARDIAN

CHLOE'S WATCHER

CHLOE'S ODYSSEY

THE CLONE'S MOTHER

BABIES BY THE LITTER

going from nothing to everything
in less than sixty seconds

A memoir by
CHERI GILLARD

Published in the United States, by Cheri Gillard Publishing, www.cherigillard.com.

Cheri Gillard, 1962–
TITLE: Babies by the Litter: going from nothing to everything in less than sixty seconds | Cheri Gillard.
DESCRIPTION: First edition. | Cheri Gillard Publishing, Colorado, 2018.
KEYWORDS: Personal Memoir | Infertility and Miscarriage | Pregnancy and Bed rest | Quadruplets and Higher multiples | Dating and Marriage | Parenting
ISBN: 1724576798
ISBN-13: 978-1724576798

Library of Congress Control Number: 2018909081

Jacket design by Spencer Gillard

In grateful appreciation to Cyndi, our NeeNee.
And
for all my children.
Now you have the whole story
of us before you,
and how you came to be ours.

CONTENTS

INTRODUCTION

NOTES ON PARENTING

Parenting—a remarkable journey. I think I survived it. Though to think I'm finished would be shortsighted. Parenting never really ends, especially when your kids move back home when things don't go as hoped with their plans. I'm just parenting differently from when they depended on me to have juice boxes at the park or put the head back on their toy that just fell off again. Part of parenting at this later stage is figuring out when it's best to keep my mouth shut or finding extra cash somehow to help with their unexpected expenses. Part of it is trusting my offspring to choose well and to release them to carry the burden of worry for me. It's different, but the role is still there. I can't relinquish all concern, even if they're under their own roofs, doing their own things, with me left out of the loop. I must find the balance. It's so different from the days when I called all the shots, like planning what socks they'd wear and when they'd use the toilet.

Back when they were little, life was hectic and hard. But now looking back, I know it was good. I wish I could go back and cuddle my little babies. Now that they're grown, it's easy for me to yearn for the early days, those difficult days when I couldn't wait for them to reach milestones so we could move on to something new. Each stage was so taxing, I just wanted relief. I didn't really know—not *really*—how precious that time was. How fleeting. Of course, we always hear older, wiser people say how fast life goes, how we need to appreciate what we have when we have it, that "youth is wasted on the young" and all that. But how in the world can a mom who hasn't slept much in months—or years even—who doesn't know how she is going to get through another day of kids taking every ounce of energy, self-control, and nurturing that she can muster, how can she sit and relish the moment and know it's precious when two of the kids are fighting again, another has a fever and just vomited all over her feet, and another's diaper just blew a leak and messed her one pair of jeans that still fits? Life as a mom is tough. Who can relish it—until it's all behind her?

Maybe the answer is in how we face each day. God was onto something when he penned, "Don't worry about tomorrow; today is bad enough." It goes something like that, anyway. It means take one day at a time. When you live that way, you don't think about how fleeting the time is mothering your little ones. You're in the moment, even if you're just trying to survive. And maybe being *in* the moment is the best way, even if you're so overwhelmed, you can't possibly treasure the experience. That is unless they've just fallen asleep and you can breathe deeply for one minute. Amazing how sweet they look when they're unconscious. But there is little time to linger. You have to move the wet clothes you forgot from the washer into the dryer and hope the dryer sheet is strong enough to cover the spoiled smell. After that, the kitchen and every crusted dish is calling your name. Those scarce seconds to treasure when they sleep are as fleeting as their dropped ice cream cone on a July sidewalk.

When my kids were toddlers, strangers would ask things that focused on future worries—trying to be helpful, no doubt.

"What are you going to do when they all start to drive?" they'd ask.

I'd smile—that smile I perfected for all those nice people who knew so much more than me—and explain that I'd prefer to spend today worrying about whether or not we'd find a public bathroom for my potty-users-in-training before they wet their Pull-Ups. I'd worry about driving when we got there.

Learning to drive seemed so far away at the time. Today it is indeed far away, but on the other side of Now. When they were toddlers, I couldn't imagine my little darlings behind the wheels of vehicles—besides their ride-in fire truck that wore two parallel dirt ruts around the backyard lawn. I was too deeply immersed in the day-to-day activities that swamped me then. I was completely dedicated to the task of getting my children nurtured and prepared for launch one day, and doing that kept my mind from being able to comprehend ten or fifteen years into the future.

Raising children was certainly nothing like I'd ever thought it would be. But then again, I'm not sure *how* I thought it would be. Growing up and moving into young adulthood, I guess I assumed like so many girls that I would one day be a mom. It never crossed my mind to consider

5

the involved difficulties, challenges, sacrifices, obstacles, disappointments—the list goes on and on of what I failed to consider. I focused on the ideal—the pretty picture of a beautifully composed postpartum mother sitting in a cozy rocker, cradling her contented newborn, a starry night outside the clean window, with peace and tranquility pervading the home. Back then I didn't know mothers didn't have clean windows.

There were times in my naiveté when I wanted five or six kids (what was I thinking?) and times when I wanted none (what was I thinking?), but I figured one day my husband and I would determine when we would have children, how many of them, and then we would proceed to accomplish our plan.

My, my. Such silly assumptions get blown away by reality, don't they? And then stick a child or two into the equation. We grownups are unrealistic enough to believe we are in control until one of those little people—or even attempts to make them—enter our lives. I've heard women say things like, "Well, we've decided after we've been married three years, we'll start our family. We'll have three kids, and I want at least two girls, and I want them to be no more than two years apart—so good for playmates, you know—and we'll live happily ever after."

Reality check. Anybody who makes plans so specific, and then actually fulfills them, is nothing but plain lucky. These fortunate people get pregnant their first tries, have picture-perfect pregnancies, "easy" deliveries, and get babies who wouldn't think of waking in the middle of the night. You know the type. When it happens to people who planned it, unfortunately, it reinforces the fallacy that they actually did it themselves, that *they* are making it happen.

Ha! It won't take long though, once those little bundles of joy hit the scene, to learn it was an illusion. Parents have never been in control. People who think they're running the show are delusional. Poor dears. They are victims, really. Statistically, someone's got to have quick success—and the lot happens to fall to those poor suckers. Puts them at a disadvantage from the start, making them think they've got power, they hold the key, they call the shots. A difficult way to start parenting. It's better to go in with your eyes open— 'cause they're probably going to stay that way for many nights to come.

When my husband, Jason, and I got married, we were silly enough to think we could plan to wait five years before having kids. As it turned out—totally by chance and a lot of hard work—we did have our children not too long after five years of marriage, but that was only after realizing we had fertility problems early on, and if we wanted kids at all, we'd better get a jump on it and start to work toward that end.

And work we did. And it paid off. We have four children—quadruplets—three boys and a girl. As they grew up, they were delightful, they were draining. They were ingenious, they were infuriating. They are blessings I wouldn't trade for the world—but I might have loaned them out for an occasional night's sleep.

Spencer holds the birthright and was proud of it when he was younger. He was firstborn by mere seconds. That was enough for him. He proclaimed early on that when Dad died, he'd be taking over the family and would be boss. That caused a little consternation among his siblings (not to mention with Dad).

His color is blue, and he will forever be associated with blue. I know that sounds strange, but each of my children has a color. By now, their DNA must surely have tinted to match their individual colors. The color assignments came about right after they got home from the hospital. I needed to know whose bottle belonged to whom because when I set down all the bottles for a round of burps, some were still three-quarters full while others had almost nothing left. For the second half of the feeding I needed to return the right bottle to the correct baby to ensure each got a full feeding. So I assigned them each a color right then. It was random. The bottles came in four main colors. Spencer happened to have a blue one at that moment, so blue became his.

With his blue clothes, blue toys, and blue everything else (though his disposition has *never* been blue), Spencer lived in a wonderful world. It wasn't our world, but it seemed to be a very exciting one. His imagination was always in high gear. I overheard him playing sometimes, saying as just a five-year-old, "I crown thee king, poor squire, and place thee upon the throne of all England." (When he played, he often spoke in the King James Version.) And then there was the time when he had no idea who that mysterious spy was who had galloped through the kitchen on his horse (when I just happened to be out of the room) and stole his homework and told him he would be forever cursed to even consider completing those evil worksheets. Alas, he was indeed a happy boy. And I was left wondering where that homework disappeared to. Today, his optimism is refreshing and a gift to me, not to mention an amazing asset as he faces the challenges millennials have these days achieving their dreams for job security and lasting relationships my own generation took for granted.

Pierce, the second in line to the throne, relinquished his position of power early on for a more peaceful kind of existence. From the time he was an infant, he sat back and watched the others play, quietly contemplating but frequently keeping at a safe distance (probably from

Spencer's unexpected sudden manifestations of medieval warriors or World War II troops).

Pierce actually has two colors, because we didn't have enough purple bottles and not everything comes in purple, while yellow seems always to be an option. His easy-going nature allowed him to accept having both yellow and purple, instead of one of the colors his brothers got that is traditionally associated with the male gender.

His nose was often in a book—and still is to this day. Frequently after a day at elementary school, when the kids were milling around the house, I would eventually notice one was missing. (At least I always had them count off before leaving the school, so I knew everyone probably made it as far as the driveway.) The missing kid was Pierce, still in the car reading, unable to stop long enough to come inside. His sense of humor was sharp, and he got things so fast. At times when I mumbled some joke that was really for me alone (when I was talking to myself to give me the illusion I could still carry on an adult conversation), Pierce would give me a sideways glance and cute little grin and quietly remark, "That's funny." Now he's transferred his love of story and literature, his insight and humor, to teaching English to high school students. When he gets home after a day of teaching, he can sit in his own driveway reading as long as he wants—until he needs to get busy grading papers, that is.

Molly is our daughter. Her color was easy to decide: red (or pink if necessary, though she preferred less dainty things than pink). Growing up, she was a little mother. When I lay down exhausted, she tended to me like an angel, brushing the hair from my forehead, asking what she could get for me. And that was when she was only three! She covered me with a blanket, rubbed my back, and brought me slippers. (Better than a puppy. *And* she was housebroken by then—more on that later.) In kindergarten on the playground, when she saw the other kids getting too rambunctious, she suggested to the playground monitor it might be a good idea to slow things down before someone got hurt. And if someone did get a scrape, she'd be there in an instant, checking to see that they were all right and to find out if they needed a band-aid. She came to me one day when Spencer was upset about something and told me before I talked to him, "Be extra careful with Spencer, Mom. He's very tender right now." She was only four. Now over two decades later, she still is a nurturing caregiver, one who is deeply, genuinely concerned and loving.

Charles, the youngest if you count seconds, is a passionate feeler. As a child, he was deep and mysterious. Often, neither he nor I was certain what was pressing at his conscience, and I had to help him explore what thoughts were hiding beneath the surface of his awareness, plaguing him or stirring him. When I heard his repeated deep sighs, I knew it was time to pursue some kind of intervention. Once when he was only five, he lamented—like the Apostle Paul had done in Romans 7—"Why do I keep sinning, doing what I don't want to do? I know what I should do, but I don't do it…." Really, I swear, he actually said that. This wasn't spewing anything back that he had heard me say. I didn't even know Paul had written about this to the church in Rome until I shared the story with some well-educated church lady at a moms' group I went to. She asked me if I had consoled Charlie with Paul's story. To have such insight! I'd been stammering for deep words of comfort like, "Oh, I bet Bert and Ernie have trouble keeping their toys picked up too." True to his DNA, he remains a deep feeler, thinker, and a bit of a mystery. His perfectionism drives him forward; he must do well and accomplish as much as he possibly can. (Speaking of his DNA, Charlie's color is green.)

The adventure of watching these four young fascinating beings grow into the complex adults that they now are has been an incredible ride and a blessing beyond expression. It's been a pure delight and an amazing experience as I've penned this memoir to reflect on my children whom I once knew so well, little people I used to spend practically every single day with, day in and day out, for a solid eighteen years. What a process it has been to put together our story and recount the journey that brought us to where we are now. And what a journey it has been!

But I'm jumping ahead. Let's go back, and I'll tell you how it all started.

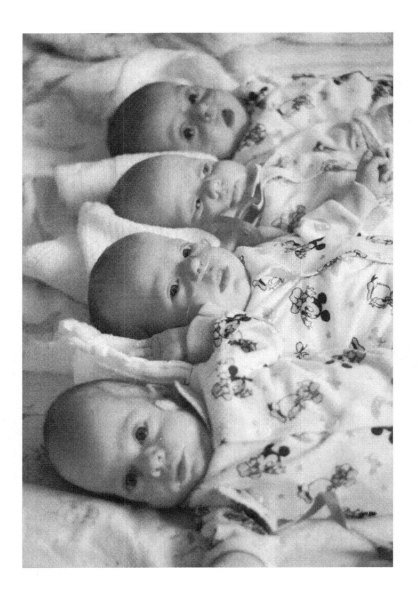

CHAPTER 1

THE BIRDS AND THE BEES

My children are test tube babies. That used to be pretty remarkable, but these days it's not that uncommon. Now there are so many children resulting from the many new methods to get babies, the lessons don't always apply anymore when you read educational books to your kiddos about special marriage hugs or cuddles that result in children. So often those particular hugs and cuddles fail miserably to produce a baby. And now, not only are there youngsters whose beginnings were in laboratories, but sometimes the babies don't belong biologically to their dads, or even to the surrogates they grow inside of.

We're fortunate enough that we can say our kids belong completely, utterly, and wholly to my husband and me. We were lucky enough that our doctor was able to use bits from each of us and to get them to work together to build a family for us. We just had to do it unconventionally.

So from diapers to braces to car insurance to college tuition, they and their DNA have been all ours. When they were young and curious, I wanted to do my best when the time came for the "Big Question." You know the one. *Where do babies come from?* I was determined to be ready the first time they asked, "Mom, how do you make a baby?" I thought long and hard about how to address this issue ahead of time. The professionals tell us to be honest and straightforward. Books teach us to use anatomically correct language. Look them in the eye, and for heaven's sake, don't blush. We don't want to start them out with the misconception that sexuality is something to be embarrassed about, now do we?

Almost looking forward to the opportunity, I was prepared to make healthy, well-adjusted little people of my children and to help them understand that, even though their conception was unusual, they were cherished. I didn't want them to feel abnormal because they were conceived in a lab with Mom and Dad nowhere in sight. As a nurse, I was ready to use printed visual aids and vocabulary lists—anything that would help them learn the facts in the most comfortable, safe environment I could provide.

On the day the question first came up, it was at the dinner table. Of course it was at the dinner table. That's where we've had so many of our family discussions. How natural for the kids to question the genesis of our very beings around mashed potatoes, peas, and chicken. With the potatoes as an ovum and peas as sperm, we had on our dinner plates all the tools I would need to demonstrate the physiological process of egg fertilization. When finished, we could even enter into a philosophical discussion about if the chicken came before the ovum or not.

So, when I looked out at four pairs of expectant eyes after the innocent yet meteoric question was uttered, trying to put together the words that would forever shape their impression of who and why they are…I chickened out.

"Well, you see, it was like this. Because things didn't work right, I went to the doctor and he gave me lots of medicine. And Dad gave me shots everyday until my body made a bunch of eggs. When they were ready, I went into the operating room and the doctor took the eggs out of my body. Then he mixed them in a little dish with little parts, kind of like eggs, from Dad, and they joined up and made tiny little babies. They floated around for a few days in the little dish until they were strong enough, then I returned to the operating room and the doctor put them back inside me. Then they stayed there for the rest of the time until you were ready to be born. Then I went back into the operating room and the doctor cut my tummy open and took you out, and here you are. Now, eat your potatoes."

That didn't fly. I had to tell them more. Especially Molly. For the boys, after a few key questions were answered, they shrugged it off and restarted their discussion for plans to play in the backyard with their shovels after dinner. But with Molly, we had to have additional meetings afterwards just to begin to cover her endless questions. And believe me, her interrogation wasn't satisfied until after I got out charts and graphs and did a lot of explicit explaining.

But to be honest, I wouldn't have been satisfied either with some cockamamie story about a dish and some speck-sized babies swimming around. I would want to know, like Molly did, *how* did the doctor get the eggs out, *how* did he get them back in, and just *what* has Dad got to do with all this?

As test-tube babies, my children weren't typically conceived, not by a long shot. No memorable romantic interlude to recall as the unquestionable moment that love and tenderness resulted in the creation of new life. Way too many people were involved in the process for intimate, private recollection. One day I was driving with my mother past the surgical center where I'd had the procedures that eventually resulted in my pregnancy. I said to her, "Hey, there's the building where my kids were conceived. I bet there aren't many people who can point to a public building and say that."

With a mischievous smile, she answered, "Well, you never know...."

Omigosh! What was my mother revealing? She was teasing. Had to be. *My* mother? It was a joke, I'm sure of it. *La la la,* with fingers in my ears—as best as I could while still driving. I banished those thoughts, put aside any imaginings of what she might be suggesting, and I drove on, never mentioning such scandalous things again.

As expected, questions about the Birds and the Bees came up again later with my kids. More than once. One must offer as much, but not too much, of what a child is ready to hear, which inevitably prolongs the teaching process about procreation over many years. It's important to offer information as they grow. Whether you like it or not. If you want well-rounded kids with healthy sexuality and identity, you have to keep talking about it.

I had to wonder after our initial lessons just what the kids took away from them. Though it's probably easier to tell children everything when they're young enough to shrug it off, not really grasping what you're saying, they haven't truly heard you until you get a reaction of *some* sort. I discovered, unfortunately, there isn't a lot of retention when boys are busy trying to wolf down their chicken and mashed potatoes so they can get back outside and dig more holes in the backyard. But as time went forward, with the occasional opportunity, I filled in some blanks, including a few of the details of their own unusual conception because the conventional methods didn't work for us.

One Advent season, a year or so after their initial inquiry, we had an unplanned pop quiz of sorts after church to check how well my teaching was going.

Our pastor Bill was preaching a sermon series over the month of December highlighting the different people who took part in the first Christmas story. The first Sunday of Advent, he told about the Virgin Mary and what she must have experienced when she encountered the angel and all that followed. He explained the Virgin Mary's circumstances, the Virgin Mary's probable age, and the Virgin Mary's position in society. He described what it would have meant for this young woman, the Virgin Mary, to find herself pregnant without a husband. He talked us through what it might have been like for the Virgin Mary to have to break the news of her condition to Joseph, her fiancé.

About halfway through the sermon, after Pastor Bill had mentioned the word *virgin* at least 999 times, I leaned over to my friend and said, "My kids are going to want to know what a virgin is when we get home."

She smiled and said with all the confidence of a mother with older kids, "A young girl. Just tell them it's a young girl."

I wasn't as certain as she seemed to be that the "young girl" explanation was going fly, especially with Molly.

I didn't have to wait long to find out that I was correct.

As the kids and I walked the corridor from the sanctuary toward the exit, about one half minute out of the service, the first of my children posed the question: "What's a version?"

"A young girl." He said no more. Phew. That was easy after all.

Then one who was up ahead came back and asked, "What's a ver...ver...verjun, or whatever that was?"

"A young girl." Two down.

Then Molly decided she wanted to know. And when Molly wants to know, Molly makes sure she finds out.

"What's a virgin?"

"A young girl," I tried.

"What do you mean? Dad said it was someone who hadn't had children yet."

Dang. He and I should have gotten our stories straight before we left the pews. Now I knew there would be no leaving it like that. But I wanted the freedom to speak freely and not be overheard by the church ladies standing at the coffee and cookie table.

"We're almost to the car. I can tell you about it on the way home," I said.

Jason had driven separately. I was on my own.

Once to the car, Molly sat up front to be sure she didn't miss a single word.

I said, "Remember me telling you that when a couple has a Special Hug to show they love each other and to start a baby? Well, a virgin is someone who has never done that."

"Now, how is it again that the sperm gets to the egg?" Charlie asked from behind me.

He'd been listening better than I thought. Of course. Perfectionist Charlie.

I told them what happened during the Special Hug that allowed fertilization, implantation, and so forth. And of course, Molly wanted to discuss the social aspects, the reality that some teenagers do that before they are married. She restated how they make bad choices, and that's why some of them have babies. Then she wanted to know *why* someone would *want* to do *that*. Meanwhile, the boys who

18

sat in the back of the van chimed in their questions here and there when they needed some clarification.

So I explained in greater detail than ever before how once a person starts to grow up and their hormones and bodies change, they want to be closer to someone they love, and when they have a Special Hug, it feels good to them and they like it.

Well, Molly wanted—*needed*—to understand *how* it felt.

I, on the other hand, wanted—*needed*—to stay very vague on this. I didn't want to get into any detailed descriptions. So I tried the elusive approach and didn't answer her in any more detail than I already had. "It feels good to them," I said. But she kept at it.

"But *how* does it feel? Don't you understand me? You just don't get it. *What* does it *feeeeel* like? Don't you understand what I'm asking?"

I tried to answer her, speaking very deliberately in third person. "Well, people like the way it feels, because it feels good—physically. It is pleasant for them."

Molly finally realized I was balking and said, "Are you feeling uncomfortable with this? Because if you are, we can talk about it more later in private." Truly. Her words.

I told her, "It's a very private thing for people. I'm not sure about explaining details to you."

At this point, Spencer—who'd been listening from his seat in the far back of the van—finally chimed in and admonished Molly. He was very relaxed as he spoke, his hands clasped behind his head and his elbows out as he reclined a bit in the seat. (He was obviously very sure of himself.) "Molly, why are you bugging *her* so much about it anyway? She wouldn't know. She's never done it."

I had to concentrate not to swerve off the road or laugh out loud. He was so comfortably confident that *his* mom had never done *that*.

"Why do you say that, Spencer?" I asked as casually as I could.

"*You* told me."

"I did?"

"Yeah. You said it wouldn't work for you to have a baby like that so you had to go to the doctor and let him help you have one."

I guess this is what I get for avoiding the full truth the first time. First impressions can be lasting, and apparently everything I mentioned after that initial "doctor and dish" story was dismissed because Spencer was relieved to know his mother was happily safe from those mysteries I described.

As we drove on, the boys continued to bombard me with inquiries about the logistical aspects of the entire thing while discussing among themselves their own perceptions and hypotheses of how this act could be accomplished. One of the truths they figured out was how difficult the whole phenomenon could be because of clothing. They had many creative ideas of how one would do this. After Spencer suggested to his brothers that he thought one reason for zippers in pants was for this purpose, I dropped the bomb that couples wanted to be as close as possible and they didn't mind having the Special Hug without clothes on.

This left them stunned with mouths agape and their young faces contorted in a variety of incredulous expressions.

Her brothers' silence was Molly's cue to suggest again that if I was uncomfortable discussing all this, I could wait and talk to her about it later at home in private.

Dear Molly. Her maternal instincts rivaled my own.

CHAPTER 2

NOTES ON BEING ABANDONED

1988

In these early years of hoping to have a baby, I just want to be like everyone else. Or at least what I think everyone else is like. I look longingly at others and jealously imagine—and I can admit, sure, it's a little naive—that everything in other people's lives progress just as they hope and want. As I covet their "easy" lives, I dream that I, too, might get to wake up one day and—perhaps at the breakfast table or brushing my teeth before work—unexpectedly, suddenly realize that I could be pregnant. I want it to surprisingly dawn on me that my period is late and I've forgotten to notice. This is a delusion of course. Since thirteen years of age, I haven't had a single monthly cycle which hasn't been painful or awful. I'm accustomed to being bedridden with immeasurable pain for at least one day, if not three, every month. How can I possibly miss a period unaware?

Well, if I am going to live in a dream world, I might as well make it a nice one.

Because I've always had trouble with menstruation, a doctor I saw during college warned me I would probably have difficulty getting pregnant. I've been to a fertility specialist here in Chicago to see if he can or should do anything to help. From my history, he believes I need laser laparoscopy, both for diagnosis and treatment. That's like those knee scope surgeries, only instead of inserting the instruments and camera into your knee through small incisions, they put them inside of your belly to have a look around and do any needed repair or treatment.

Jason takes the day off from work and accompanies me to Northwestern Hospital for the procedure. I couldn't ask for a more reputable place to take care of me, right? The surgery will be done outpatient, so I'm not being admitted to stay overnight. I have to check in, get my operation, recover, and check out all in one day. Insurance rules.

Everyone we meet seems friendly. They check me in and make me exchange my clothes for a white and blue hospital gown. They insert an IV into my arm and place a puffy bouffant hat over my hair. They say it's time, I say goodbye to Jason, and they roll me into the OR. It's not long and the anesthesiologist says goodnight, have a good nap, and everything fades to black.

After the surgery, I slowly come out of a drugged sleep. Someone is talking to me, calling my name, but I'm terribly groggy. And my belly throbs. They give me something for pain. I'm in and out of consciousness, wanting to just stay asleep. But they won't let me. They keep bugging me and forcing me to wake up. I wish they'd leave me alone. After an hour or so in the recovery room— I have no concept of time passage, but I know the usual course of treatment allows about an hour in recovery—my nurse and doctor are apparently satisfied with my improvement, and they decide it's time to transfer me to my room in the outpatient post-surgical ward. Once there, I see Jason for a second, quietly sitting in a chair in the corner with a book temporarily closed over his finger, while the team of experts gets me settled into my new bed.

While I'm trying to sleep off the powerful drugs they've poured into my veins, a nurse shakes me awake saying, "Cheri? Cheri, wake up." She is making sure I'll rouse after having been put under. I still want to stay asleep, but she won't let me. She takes my vital signs, checks my dressings, gives me something more for the pain, and spoons ice chips past my lethargic lips—all a part of "recovering" me from the anesthesia and surgery. She's pretty intent on interrupting my slumber, but no matter how hard she works, all I want to do is sleep. As soon as she stops fussing with me, I slip right back into a deep sleep. The repetitive cycle of her waking and pestering me seems to go on for hours and hours. After a time, the ice progresses to sips of juice, and she introduces nibbles of saltine crackers into the mix.

The lights are low in my room, and Jason continues to sit near my bedside, quietly reading by the dimming light coming through the window as the day grows long. He helps me reposition or use Chapstick or sip juice because the nurse isn't around this time when I wake up.

After another long doze, I wake up again on my own and look down at my stomach and see that blood has seeped through my hospital gown over the bandage below my belly button. "I'm bleeding," I say and ask Jason to call the nurse to come check my dressings and incision site. He pushes the call light, and when no one answers, he decides to save time and go fetch her in person.

He walks out of my room…into *darkness*. My nurse is gone. *Everyone* is gone. The overhead lights are turned off. The unit is completely empty, closed down. Not a sound. Only dim security lights glow along the hollow corridors. I've been forgotten. Abandoned.

After Jason tells me everyone is gone, he goes searching to try to find someone to help. Through the dark hallways he wanders until he finds a nearby inpatient unit with its lights still on and bustling with activity. Stopping a nurse whisking past him by the nurses' station, he tells her that his wife has had surgery but that everyone is gone, that I am over in a room, and they left me there alone. And my incision is bleeding.

If you think that gets a reaction, you're right. Patient abandonment is a pretty big deal. Hospitals and their lawyers frown on the practice. So suddenly, I sure get plenty of attention. People come, they turn the lights back on, and they take royal care of me. They work a lot harder to get me awake, drinking, eating, and moving. They finally discharge me late in the evening. They roll me in a wheelchair down to the front entrance of the hospital and help me into a taxi. Jason will take over now and get me home to convalesce there. It all works out, fortunately. I don't have any complications. I've decided not to lodge a complaint with the hospital to tell them what happened, though I probably should at least get a reduced fee for the post-op charges, since Jason (or nobody) did a lot of my recovery.

The surgery indeed confirmed the doctor's suspicion that I have endometriosis. He cauterized the numerous lesions that were splattered over the inside of my abdomen, and he removed what scarring he could from the many years of disease I've suffered. He said the whole thing (minus the patient abandonment part) was successful.

Now that the doctor has cleaned me out, to complete the treatment, he puts me on the medication Lupron. The treatment protocol will stop the regrowth of the lesions by eliminating the hormones that sustain them.

The Lupron knocks out my estrogen, putting me into immediate and extreme menopause. The greatest difficulty with the medication is the terrible side effects. For one, it makes me temporarily infertile (more than I already am). And because of the chemically induced menopause, my thermostat is thrown utterly out of whack.

It's especially hard to tolerate when I'm at work. My job is in the neonatal ICU, or NICU (pronounced "nick-you" for short) at Chicago's Children's Memorial Hospital. As I stand beneath a warming bed taking care of a critically ill infant, suddenly my new nefarious companion, the Hot Flash, sneaks up on me with abrupt, miserable fury. The heat seeps from beneath my skin and overwhelms my entire body, making me feel as though I'm wrapped in plastic and cooking from the inside out. It's terribly difficult to remain focused on my tasks, tending an extremely sick baby, as I stand burning up under the bed's heating elements that are there to keep the newborn in front of me warm.

My wonderful charge nurse, Ruth, knows about my surgery and new medication and the wicked thing it does to me. She can tell when I suddenly turn into a searing bundle of agitated heat. She steps in, takes over, and lets me walk away until the evil Flash passes and I can return to my duties. With an injection every four weeks, the treatment will last for several months—several months of pure torture. When I finish the course of meds, I will be more relieved than I can express and ready to move on to the next step of our plan to become parents.

Over these many months, our doctor sends Jason to a different doctor, a specialist who is making sure Jason is in prime shape for fatherhood. He's having his own beautiful experiences to repair or improve his chances for having kids. It *is* beautiful, right? Of course it is. Simply because it's possible to do (we must tell ourselves), and we're lucky the treatment is available to us; it's a privilege. You've got to love it. Or you might go a little crazy. Nothing is left unbothered or private, by the way. But we're still pretty tolerant. Open-minded and willing. It's not so horrible, really. I imagine we'll be sick and tired of it if it goes on for too many months. But for now, we deal with it. We're young. Resilient. Optimistic.

After the multitude of tests and procedures for both of us, our main doctor meets with us and reviews all we've been through. He flips through the many pages of our charts with our lab and test results, quickly reading the figures and notes. He proclaims all is well, and everything looks splendid now. At the conclusion of our appointment, he shakes our hands and says that he expects to see us in his office within a few months for a positive pregnancy test.

CHAPTER 3

THE BOWLING ALLEY

I love bowling, though I'm terrible at it. If I break fifty, I've had an astounding game. With baseball as the only sport I've ever followed, I've applied what I know about baseball to bowling: Strikes Are Bad. You don't want them. So I'm careful to steer clear of them. If I get a strike, it's a total fluke. Watching me bowl you'd think the goal is to throw the ball right into the gutter, sometimes with me still attached to the ball.

So if I'm so terrible, why do I love it?

Because it was at a bowling alley that our mutual friend Mary introduced Jason and me.

We were at the Marina Towers bowling alley in Chicago. (Marina Towers are those two round buildings on the Chicago River that look like corncobs.) A group of us young adult professionals from a Fourth Presbyterian

Church discussion group had an outing to go bowling one Friday evening in January of 1986. We bowled a few games, then went out afterwards to a café for hot cider or cocoa and fresh-from-the-oven cinnamon rolls.

At the restaurant, by chance as everyone encircled the table and pulled out a wooden chair, the seat I pulled out was next to the one Jason grabbed. Our proximity gave us the chance to become better acquainted. He told me a little about himself, explaining his work to me. He was a commodities broker who sold things that weren't his to other people. At least that's how I understood it. I'd never heard of the vocation before or comprehended what Futures were. I didn't know what the Board of Trade was either, or what a commodities firm did.

To help me understand, as an illustration he explained the whole business to me using a random car glistening beneath the night lights outside along the curb of Michigan Avenue. "See that car out there?" I followed his finger to look out the café plate glass window where he pointed. "I can sell it to you and collect payment, as long as you sell it again to someone else before the date arrives to take possession."

It sounded a lot like larceny and fraud to me. To think there were real companies, entire industries apparently, thriving on those preposterous principles, making many people rich in the process. It was ludicrous. I didn't get it, but I decided to take his word for it. He seemed like an honest enough guy. And he was handsome. So why not believe him?

Once we'd enjoyed our sticky buns, hot drinks, and fellowship with new friends, it was time to call an end to the evening. We all dispersed, saying good night and each going our own way. The more wealthy of the group hailed cabs while others of us hopped on the 151 Michigan

Avenue bus or headed east to the El over on State Street. It had been a nice evening. I was glad to have met Jason and wondered if I might chance to see him again. That would be fine with me.

CHAPTER 4

NOTES ON BEING OVERSTIMULATED

The doctor has given us the green light to get pregnant. We have to be intentional and methodical about achieving results. With my Lupron shots *behind me* (yep, my little attempt at a pun), I've got my hormones back. They're kind of essential to the whole pregnancy process. I have to act immediately, getting pregnant before the return of my endometriosis, a persistent adversary. The pesky condition has certainly experienced a setback with the attacks against it with both laser and drugs, but endometriosis is an issue that doesn't disappear. It's like dandelions in your lawn. You can dig them up, spray them, pull off the heads—but in a few weeks, you're going to have bright golden heads splattered across your yard again. And a yard full of dandelions isn't going to get you pregnant very easily.

The very first step is to begin the morning temperature checks to figure out my fertile days. Every single morning, day in, day out, before I budge from bed or even breathe very deeply, I reach to my bedside table—gently lest I generate activity that will raise my basal body temperature—and I pick up my thermometer and slip it under my tongue. Once it beeps, I chart the results on graph paper and track what is happening in my body. I make the graphs as interesting and fun as possible with added color and doodles. But even with what appears to be spikes in my temperature—the signal to tell when I am supposedly ovulating—they aren't enough. No success. And I'm getting tired of every stinking morning needing to take my temperature before moving. Eventually, I change to ovulation kits which are much more sensitive and accurate. But time tick-tocks and still nothing happens. Month after month passes, and I must face disappointment again and again.

More than a year later, after a stressful move and a job change, a new doctor takes over our care. She receives copies of our charts and the history of all the treatments up until this point. Looking through the labs, she finds the tests that our previous doctor had proclaimed normal and good before he sent us home to get pregnant.

She says, "He told you *what?* These tests are *so far* from normal."

She explains how Jason totally flunked his tests. They probably should make him return his diploma.

It takes a moment for what she said to sink in.

Alas, all the time wasted, those squandered attempts.

I know that sounds cynical. But when one is working

with a thermometer, graphs, and ova kits, letting *them* dictate the time and place, and not the usual romantic evening or intimate morning interlude, one begins to see intimacy as one thing only—a means to an end, a project, a chore. It is not uncommon to hear infertile couples telling stories of dropping everything for a midday rendezvous to allow Mr. Sperm to be introduced to Miss Ovum, who is on a very tight schedule and can't be put off, even if Mr. Sperm is in a meeting and needs to excuse himself. She only has hours to live and must not be kept waiting. It tends to diminish the intimacy in a relationship. It's been known too many times to drive couples to divorce.

As time passes and after I undergo even more procedures, we move again and change doctors yet one more time. We start seeing another specialist who recognizes neither of us is a prime example of raging fertility. He suggests we waste no more time with conservative treatments and let him "shoot with both barrels"—since ours are blanks, so to speak. First, he recommends that I have laser surgery again to clean out the endometriosis that has grown back since the first surgery, which was about three years ago now. Then he recommends that we do a procedure called "ZIFT"— Zygote Intrafallopian Transfer. It is the cutting edge treatment these days. The eggs and sperm are put into a Petri dish like with *in vitro* fertilization. But to increase the odds of success, after fertilization and a few days to grow, the little tadpoles are transferred directly inside the fallopian tubes instead of the uterus because normal fertilization takes place in the tubes, thus increasing the likelihood of implantation. It means I'll have an incision for the procedure, but I'm not daunted by that. I've been cut open before. I've been an OR nurse. People get cut open all the time. We are up for that. We're all in. Let's do this!

We start by signing over everything we own to the doctor—savings, checking, savings bonds, 401k plans, rights to our firstborn. Using both barrels will take a lot of money. A *lot* of money. Oh, well. What do we need with cash? Do we truly require a house, a car, a nest egg, or even lunch money? We'll only really need those things if the process works and we end up with a kid, right? A kind of Catch 22. But the odds for success aren't great anyway. And if by some miracle a baby does show up, a little rented apartment and one old car might get us by. We'll cross that bridge if we ever get to it.

While processing all the information and preparing for the entire course of treatment—what risks it brings, how much cash it requires, and what the possible outcomes are—I write to Jeanne, my friend in Chicago, to tell her about what we're doing and what it involves. In the letter, I explore for the first time what, in theory, could happen, and it makes it so much clearer and more real as I put it down in ink on paper. I start out being silly at first, then the truth of it dawns on me in a new way as I share my thoughts with her.

"...maybe we'll get two for the price of one. Maybe three? Four? Oh, boy. Actually, twenty percent of the pregnancies from ZIFT are multiple gestation. I could handle twins, but no more. Too scary."

First, I go through the laser laparoscopy surgery again. They say it takes only a few days to recover, but in reality it takes a lot longer to feel better. The worst part of the recovery is dealing with the pain caused by being inflated with carbon dioxide gas. They fill you with it like a beach ball to puff you up so everything inside is visible, but really!

Can a body feel normal in "only a few days" after something like that?

After a few weeks, once I finally do recover, it's time to start the specific steps to prepare for the ZIFT procedure. It's Tuesday, February 4, 1992, and the doctor puts me back on that nasty Lupron. He assures me that since it is only short term, it won't render me infertile, and there won't be time for me to develop hot flashes. It will act short-term to knock out my usual hormones that might try to have ideas of their own while the doctor manipulates my systems to make them cooperate with his plans.

After lessons from the doctor's office nurse on how to give me shots at home, Jason starts giving me daily injections of Pergonal and Metrodin, medications to cause more eggs to mature than the usual one per month.

I'm starting to have pain in my ovaries after only five days of getting the new drugs. The doctor says it's a result of "socking it to them" with such potent drugs. I am having frequent blood tests and ultrasounds to monitor my progress to make sure everything is okay. These drugs are powerful, and we're finding that I'm ultra sensitive to them, responding rapidly, making plenty of eggs—many more than most women produce on the medication. Besides the sore hips from all the needle sticks, I continue to get more bloated with abdominal tenderness every day. Something major is going on inside of my body.

Exactly thirty-five hours before the scheduled egg retrieval, Jason gives me a special shot, a drug called Profasi, that will cause all the matured eggs to prepare for launch. He gives it to me at 11:00 p.m. on Saturday evening, February 22.

Thirty-five hours later, I go into the operating room, waving goodbye to Jason as they roll me away. It's time for the doctor to perform the egg retrieval. You don't want to know how that gets done because it involves a needle about as big as a fishing rod. And coincidently, I got to see it when I woke up in the middle of the procedure. *Eeek.* I don't think that is a normal part of the plan. The anesthesiologist responded so quickly to put me back under that I figure he didn't mean for me to wake up. As he eased me back down after I sat up with a start, he said, "Oh, you're feeling some pain there? Let me help you with that…." I went back to sleep and didn't wake up again until they wanted me to, and by then, everything was finished.

With the fishing rod, they've sucked out twenty-three eggs total. Now the eggs are mixed in a fine solution of concentrated sperm and my own blood that they drew earlier—a good medium to use, they tell me. Everyone is settled down for a long winter's nap in a dark warm Petri dish. Or at least for a couple of days. We go home to wait. (Test tube babies aren't made in test tubes, by the way. That just sounds nicer than Petri dish babies. The alliteration rings better, I guess.)

Forty-eight hours later, we get the phone call to come back in. The guppies are ready for transfer. That means a scalpel this time, not just a fishing rod needle. A two-inch incision in my lower abdomen allows the doc to find my fallopian tubes and place four embryos inside each tube. (Our doctor's infertility practice doesn't have cryopreservation yet, meaning he can't freeze and preserve any embryos for later use.) Once all the tiny babies are inside of me, it's time to return home, recuperate, and wait for something to happen.

It doesn't take long.

After a tough 24 hours, I am lying on the couch sipping a little chicken noodle soup from a cup Jason prepared for me, feeling pretty lousy from the surgery but trying to rest and recover my strength and mobility, when without any warning whatsoever it begins. Sudden, extreme vomiting. And it's constant. When I go to the doctor's office the next morning to have the staples removed from my incision, the nurse guesses the vomiting is from a urinary tract infection (UTI) that I must have picked up from the catheter put into my bladder during surgery. I have no other symptoms of a UTI, but that is her best working hypothesis. I don't buy it, but I'm in no condition to argue. She sets me up with antibiotics and sends me back home with Jason.

By the next morning, I can't lie down because of the increasing pressure in my abdomen, back, and chest. It's starting to get hard...to breathe...from the tension...building inside of me. All night, I vomited, unable to keep anything down, including the antibiotics, or even water. Jason calls the doctor, who happens to be out of town, so Jason tells the answering service he needs the doctor to call us right away, something is very wrong with me. We wait a few minutes and he calls us back. After Jason explains the situation, the doctor tells us to go back to his office, and his nurse will give me an antiemetic injection to stop the vomiting.

Crumpled in the backseat of the car, I retch the entire twenty-minute drive, a terrible experience that pulls on the newly closed incision of my recently opened belly. When we arrive at the doctor's office, the office nurse takes one look at me and recognizes immediately that I am not faring well. She sends me directly to the emergency room across the street for IV hydration and antibiotics to help me get over my suspected UTI. Just like the nurse, everyone at the ER thinks with a little fluid and medication, I should be feeling better soon.

Unfortunately, they are wrong. So wrong.

The more fluid they pour into my veins, the worse I

feel. They do some blood work which comes back with a profoundly elevated white blood count. They do an ultrasound that shows I am developing ascites—fluid accumulating in my abdominal cavity—and my liver is enlarged. I'm getting more and more miserable. The pressure is increasing inside of my chest and abdomen. I can barely hold still for an ultrasound. It's like I can't lie down far enough, I feel so bad but can't find a position that gives relief. I writhe about on the gurney, trying to find a comfortable place, but there is none. No one knows what is going wrong with me. Based on my elevated white cell counts, they think I must have an infection somewhere, still hanging on to that stupid UTI theory. But this feels so much worse than that. Nothing they do helps. The pain is growing, as is my belly, which is getting tighter and more distended. The more they treat me, the worse I get.

They page my infertility doctor for a consultation. They exchange ideas and he lets them in on the worst case scenario that could happen with the procedure he'd just put me through. With this new information, my new doctors in the emergency room start to consider that I might have ovarian hyperstimulation syndrome, a rare reaction to Pergonal which involves dangerously high estrogen levels that swell the ovaries so large they often rupture. Plus, the complication does a number on several other systems of the body.

With my labs abnormal and rapidly worsening, my condition deteriorating before their eyes, my doctors have no better ideas and admit me to the hospital.

Cheri on night shift in the NICU of Children's Memorial Hospital

CHAPTER 5

THE VALENTINE'S SPECIAL

January 1986, the month when Jason and I met at the bowling alley, was an unforgettable month—not just for the two of us but for the entire country. Though it may be hard to imagine with the way they're playing now, the Chicago Bears won the Super Bowl. I was not a football fan, and when the Bears fans took to the streets that night cheering and partying after they won the championship, they woke me up eleven stories above them in my high-rise apartment on the corner of Chicago Avenue and Dearborn Street. I was sleeping between night shifts at the hospital, and I wasn't amused.

Two days later in a horrific national and human tragedy that shook us all to the core, the Challenger Space Shuttle, with the teacher Christa McAuliffe aboard, exploded seventy-three seconds after takeoff. When I woke up late that afternoon after another night shift, a friend told me what had happened. I kept waiting for the punch line to the sick joke. I couldn't believe he was telling the truth.

He kept saying, "No, it really happened. I'm not joking. It's real. It happened."

We were stunned, shocked. Eyes locked to the TV screens showing the replay over and over of the trail of white smoke in the sky splitting apart into two billowing horns, we tried to wrap our heads around this horrendous catastrophe.

In the days that followed, as the shock abated and we tried to accept what had happened, time marched forward and dragged us along with it—though our conversations often went back to that heartbreaking event for a long while. One of my activities of normalcy was to participate in the dinner group club we had through Fourth Presbyterian Church. Eight to ten of us "yuppies" were in each group, and we met weekly at different restaurants around Chicago for a month to have dinner and get to know each other. Then after a month together, the coordinator reassigned us, and we met with a different combination of people. Jason and I were put in the same dinner group for the month of February. With our first two meetings, we became more acquainted with each other along with all the others in the group. No clairvoyant sense alerted me, no bolt of lightning zapped me to tell me that I was looking at my future husband. We just visited like everyone else. When our second dinner was wrapping up, everyone in the group agreed to meet again the next Tuesday at D.B. Kaplan's, a great delicatessen with over 150 sandwiches on its menu located on the seventh floor of Water Tower Place. (I always had The Californian, a hot open-faced sandwich with melted Monterey Jack and cheddar over turkey, tomatoes and avocados, plus toasted almonds. Doesn't that make you hungry?)

Two days after that second dinner gathering, I was working on a Thursday night before my weekend off. During the shift, I got the idea that, with a Friday night looming and an entire weekend off for myself, I wanted to go see a movie. Then I thought it would be more fun not to do it alone. Then the inspiration evolved to ask Jason if he would like to come along. (Coincidentally, that Thursday night shift was dawning onto the morning of Friday, February 14, Valentine's Day—which had less to do with my plan than the fact that it was a Friday night and I had the weekend off. Really.)

I'd learned enough about him to know that he left his apartment on the far north side in Rogers Park to take the El to the Loop rooster-crowing early. So around 5:30 a.m., I plopped down at the desk phone in my hospital unit (fortunately, I had a light patient load that night) and rang up his number that I found in the dinner group roster. No answer. After a couple more tries, I realized I'd called too late and missed him. So I'd have to catch him at work. Unfortunately, the roster didn't have work phones listed. When I got home minutes before 8:00 a.m., I pulled out the big old phonebook. Flipping through, I located the commodities firm Merrill Lynch and found a whole column of numbers. I chose the one that looked closest to the department Jason had described as his own and called. A pleasant fellow answered, and I asked if Jason worked there. He didn't know him, so I described what he did to the best of my understanding, leaving out that I'd thought the whole thing seemed an awful lot like larceny and fraud. The nice man said he thought that sounded like one particular department, so he transferred me there. I waited on hold a few minutes. When another kind clerk answered, I explained again that I was looking for Jason and wondered if he might work in his department. The name didn't immediately ring any bells for him. He asked what Jason looked like. I told him and he asked around his co-workers. One guy thought he knew him from another floor. Everyone was delightfully congenial and eager to help. After spending a few minutes on hold again, another friendly voice answered. After we talked for a bit, he tilted away his receiver and shouted out to his co-workers, asking if anyone knew Jason and took suggestions of where to call next. We did it all once more. But after several transfers and many additional amicable interactions, I still hadn't found Jason. It had gotten late enough that I could finally call a friend in the dinner group and see if she had his work number.

She rustled through her papers. Yep, she'd found it. "Ready?" She read it to me.

"Thanks. I've been calling all over Merrill Lynch looking for him."

"Cheri, he doesn't work at Merrill Lynch."

"He doesn't?"

"No," she said. "He works at PaineWebber.

Hmm. Well, that explained why I couldn't find him at Merrill Lynch. At least they were all very cordial there and didn't seem to mind trying to help.

With my newly gained information, and dialing the correct company this time, I found Jason on the second ring.

I said, "Hey, I'm going to go to a movie tonight and maybe get some dinner. Do you want to come with me?"

"Sure."

I had been so absorbed trying to find him, I hadn't thought or planned further than that. I was blank. I didn't have a movie picked out or a restaurant chosen. Clearly, I wasn't very good at asking someone out.

So he called out to his co-workers and asked for suggestions for a place to have dinner.

"The Green Door Tavern," answered Courtney, one of the other commodity guys.

Sounded great to both of us. "Any movie ideas?" Jason added to the room.

"That new Woody Allen one, *Hannah and Her Sisters?*" a man named Scott suggested.

Neither of us were fans of Woody, but Scott assured us it was getting good reviews.

So, we had a plan. It was a date.

Those commodity fellows—whether Merrill Lynch or PaineWebber guys—were the most courteous, over-the-top helpful people you'd ever want to talk to.

CHAPTER 6

NOTES ON BEING A WATER BALLOON

Over the past *four* days I've gained *thirty-five pounds*—entirely from the fluid collecting in my abdomen. Because I'm certainly not eating. The vomiting continues constantly. As the doctors and nurses pour IV fluid into my veins, it immediately leaks out through my failing vessel walls and seeps into my tissue, puffing me up like a giant water balloon. I look seven months pregnant due to the water accumulating in my belly. Because of the fluid pressure inside my skin, water is leaking out all of the injection sites from the many shots I've had. You know those cartoons where Elmer Fudd shoots his nemesis, Bugs Bunny, full of buckshot? Then Bugs takes a drink and all the liquid spews right out of the bullet holes like he's a fountain? That's how I am, only I am not as cute as the bunny.

My kidneys have started to shut down and they've stopped making urine. Which to me doesn't seem so bad because I can't get up to use the bathroom anyway. It's one less thing to worry about when I spend all day barfing into a bucket. But the doctors and nurses are getting more worried because when your systems start to shut down, it's simply a very bad thing. Meanwhile, the pain in my body is intense. They give me Demerol every three hours through my IV, but the pain relief only lasts about half way to the next dose—and I'll get that on time only if my nurse isn't too busy and stays right on top of my situation, planning ahead so she can bring my medication as soon as three hours have passed.

Every time the nurse pushes in the syringe plunger to give me the pain med, the fluid burns through my vein like fire shooting up my arm. She's started pushing it in more slowly, but it still feels like chemical heat searing my limb. My veins can't tolerate the caustic effect and they are getting chemically cauterized into oblivion. They are disappearing, turning into useless, rigid cords that will be reabsorbed over time, leaving no trace where the network of purple lines once laced beneath the surface of my thin, pale skin. Because each IV site can't hold up for more than one or two doses of Demerol, I must get a new IV placed nearly every time they give it to me. Finally, with no veins left to use, the consulting nephrologist—a kidney specialist brought in to manage my care—decides it is time to put in a subclavian catheter, a tube that will go directly into my heart. Having it will eliminate the constant needle sticks plus secure an access line in case my condition bottoms out and they need to give emergency drugs fast.

I don't need to go to the OR for the procedure. They will establish a sterile field and do the operation right here in my hospital room, in my bed. Everyone puts on surgical caps and masks, though I don't because I'm going to be under the sterile drapes. They cover me up completely, except for a small circle cutout in the blue drape that leaves my collarbone exposed. Jason is sitting next to my hospital bed, his arm stretched out to hold my hand under the surgical covers. The liquid they sponge over my skin is cold and drippy. Then a sting comes of local anesthetic to numb it. They'll keep me awake so I won't have to miss any of the fun.

To thread the central line into the right location, they have to tilt me upside down into something called Trendelenburg position. My bed is tipped so that my head is much lower than my feet, which helps make it easier to advance the guide wire into my heart. By some great mercy—it must truly be a miracle—I've stopped barfing, even upside-down, long enough that they can get started.

First the doctor inserts a wire above my clavicle and threads it through the large subclavian vein until it reaches my heart. Then he slips the catheter over the wire, removes the wire, and presto. I have a new central line.

As the doctor is working, from beneath the surgical drape I hear him say, "She won't stop bleeding. What are her clotting factors? Are her clotting times off?" No one knows, but they're commenting on how much blood I'm losing. Jason keeps a tight grip on my hand, watching the whole thing from where he is sitting on the sidelines. We wait in silence, hoping the doctor gets the situation under control. He keeps working as quickly as he can, trying to suture the tube in place and stop the bleeding. By the time he finishes and removes the surgical drapes, I'm lying in a blood-soaked bed.

Before they can use the line, they need an x-ray to confirm the correct position of the tube in my heart. After that, I can thankfully get a dose of pain med administered through the new access line. My nurse and the x-ray tech roll me onto the film plate and the big portable machine hovers over me, whirring and clicking. They take a picture of my chest. While we wait for the film to be developed, the nurses work together to change my bloody bed, not the easiest thing to do with me unable to get out. While Jason stays out of their way but never goes too far from my side, they roll me from one side to the other, pushing the lump of soiled sheets beneath me, washing me, then smoothing out new clean sheets. They put a new gown on and tuck me back in, cleaned up, and somehow, still miraculously, not throwing up.

It is not long after they finish and I am trying to catch my breath when word comes back that the catheter is not in my heart where it is supposed to be. They can't use it. We all let out a deep sigh of frustration. The line needs to be unsutured and removed and we will have to do it all over again.

Once again, with my head tipped toward the floor, the doctor covers me in drapes and swabs off the other collarbone with amber Betadine antiseptic. Jason sits next to my bed again, his arm slipped beneath the sterile drapes laying over my head and chest, holding my hand. After the doctor numbs my skin on this other side, he makes an incision and inserts the wire that will hopefully guide the long flexible tube down my blood vessels and through my chest into my heart. But this time, I feel the wire advancing inside of me. And this time, I feel it going up my neck and into my head. It has turned upward and it's going past my ear toward my brain!

"It's going up my neck!" I quickly, nervously call out from under the surgical drapes.

He tugs back the wire.

"Okay, keep telling me what you feel, if you feel it in your neck again," he instructs and he tries advancing the wire a second time.

"Yes. It's in my ear!"

We do it several more times.

"Stretch your neck and turn your head slightly to the left," he tells me. Then he has me try another way, attempting to get the wire to turn where he wants it to.

It's completely freaking me out that I can feel this foreign object moving through my body. And it's especially scary that it's in my neck, near my ear, and I can feel it sneaking toward my brain.

I'm trying to do exactly what he tells me to do, to stretch my neck just right, to tilt my head precisely like he wants, to get the invasive wire to stay out of my brain.

Suddenly, I feel a pop in the center of my chest, in the middle of my heart.

"It's in my heart. It just popped inside my heart!"

"Good," he says satisfactorily. "That's where we want it."

While I try to stay calm, breathing slow and steady to keep from screaming and going totally berserk, the doctor advances the catheter tube over the wire. After he withdraws the wire, he sutures the catheter into place so it won't move or come out. He pulls off the drapes and the nurses help clean up the mess all over again while the x-ray tech comes back in with his portable machine and takes more pictures.

This time the placement is good, something we are optimistically expecting, especially since I felt exactly where it went.

Right after that, my vomiting starts up again. Pretty crazy.

As the days wear on, my other doctor—the one who came at us with both barrels and we'd signed over our future to—tells me between my painful retches, "This will probably get a lot worse before it gets better." No sugar coating. He's being straight with me.

And it turns out, he is right.

The next night, I wake up gasping for air. My oxygen saturation has dropped into the seventy percent range, rather than the usual nineties, and the monitor alarm is shrilling through my quiet hospital room. After consulting a doctor on the phone, my nurse sends me to the radiology department for a middle-of-the-night x-ray photo shoot to find out what is going on. When I lie down flat on their table for one of the pictures, I black out. The tech grabs my arm and lifts me up and I come back. We struggle through and get the rest of the films taken, but with several more incidents where I start to lose consciousness, they realize they must keep my head elevated to keep me awake.

With the new x-rays, they discover pleural effusions. My chest has filled with the fluid that's been invading my abdomen for days. My body can't contain the liquid in my belly so it has seeped up into my lungs. It's like I'm drowning from the inside out. I am suffocating. With the head of my bed cranked up and wearing an oxygen mask, the situation seems to stabilize for now. I muster what courage and strength I can to weather this new complication.

The vomiting continues for six days and nights straight. The upmost on my mind is pain control and breathing. Of course, I can't even think of eating. Hunger is not a part of the equation. But Jason needs to eat. Though he stays by my side nearly the entire time, most nights sleeping on the hospital floor next to my bed, getting up many times to help me when I vomit, need to move, or have any other urgency, he only leaves me after the sun rises to go back to our apartment to shower, check the mail, and eat a bowl of cereal. When he returns, he stays with me in my room except for occasional trips to the cafeteria or down the hall to have a change of scenery for a few minutes. He never complains but I think he's probably tired of hearing me wretch by now. At least, after this long there is nothing to throw up. I'm having dry heaves. Ugh.

A woman who I don't know comes into my room and sits in the chair at the foot of my bed without saying much. Eventually, I learn she is a friend of my mom's. Obviously, she is there to be a support to my parents and pray for me. If she doesn't mind me barfing in my bucket constantly, I guess I don't mind the prayers. But I think I'd be more comfortable if she sat outside my door so she wouldn't hear me be sick. I'm not in a place to try to stifle my misery for the sake of a stranger.

My infertility doctor comes in every day and lingers at my bedside wringing his hands with a mournful face. He's not used to his fertility patients being sick. We're supposed to get pregnant and be happy.

The quality of treatment I receive in the hospital varies, depending on who is taking care of me. Jason does as much as he can to help, but there is only so much he can do himself. Some of the nurses and techs who care for me are wonderful—compassionate and attentive. But with others, the quality of care isn't always reliable or even seemingly competent.

Tonight, I'm finding I've drawn the short straw for nurses. My pain medication has worn off and I need another dose. I hope that if I can get the pain back under control maybe I will be able to go to sleep for a little while before throwing up more or before the pain relief wears off again. I push the button to my call light. I am waiting and waiting, but my nurse doesn't come. The pain grows, as does my anxiety and stress. When she finally appears, I swear, she doesn't know a thing about me or the care I'm supposed to get. Two hours have passed since change of shift and she supposedly got Report from my previous nurse. But not only does she know nothing about me and my condition, I have to wonder if she even knows an iota about being a nurse.

I tell her I need a dose of pain medication.

She says, "Oh? Are you in pain?"

"Yes!" I snap too quickly. I'm totally out of patience with the pain growing. I'm not able to rein in my emotions or be very gentle. "I've gained over thirty pounds in the last few days," I say desperately, trying to convey how extreme my situation is.

"Oh?" she says again, almost like she was stalling for time. "You've been eating a lot?"

"No, I've been throwing up for six days."

"So," says she, "you're not eating?"

She must have bought her nursing license from the back of a comic book. Can someone really be so dumb? Did she swipe someone's ID and sneak into the hospital as an imposter? She is pushing me past my ability to be civil.

Once she finally understands enough to realize my recent dietary habits take a backseat to all of my other problems, she leaves me to go get my meds. While I wait for her, somehow I'm lucky enough to doze, completely exhausted from so many days of barfing and misery. Suddenly, the door to my room slams open and the overhead lights blaze on.

"It's time for vitals," some young woman in a uniform announces from the doorway.

Shielding my eyes from the sudden light singeing my retinas, I mutter, "Huh?"

"Vitals. It's time to take your vitals." She's a nurse's aide, going around tormenting patients because they're trying to sleep. She comes the rest of the way into the room, banging my bedside table to a position that apparently more suits her purpose. After she jams the thermometer beneath my tongue and checks my blood pressure, pulse, and respirations, she decides now would be a good time to freshen the water in my pitcher and put out clean towels for tomorrow. Or today, now that we're in the early dark hours of the morning.

I'm remembering my first nursing job when I worked the evening shift, working till around midnight when I handed off my patient load each night shift to two veteran nurses. These lovely ladies taught me how to manage patients after bedtime. They did their night nursing almost entirely by flashlight. They snuck into rooms as quietly as church mice and, with as few disruptions as possible, they slipped blood pressure cuffs onto sleeping patients, spoke in hushed whispers, and caused only what was absolutely necessary in the way of disturbances. The floor under their care was serene, quiet, and conducive to the restful environment needed for healthful healing.

From this school of thought my rambunctious nurse's aide is not.

Once she finishes tormenting me and finally turns the light back off and leaves—with a promise to check on that pain med I've been waiting for—I try to calm down and find the least miserable position in my lumpy hospital bed while I wait for my nurse to come back.

It isn't until 3:00 a.m. that she finally brings me my pain med. When she returns, I ask her to please bring me my 4:00 a.m. antibiotic now, too, so she won't have to wake me up again in an hour to give it to me, just in case I can fall asleep.

She is so bent out of shape that I would want the medication early, she exclaims, "That's too early. It's an hour too early."

I tell her that if I were taking it at home, I would fluctuate by an hour if I needed to.

"Oh? You're taking this at home?" she questions incredulously.

Give me a break! When I finally convince her that I am not taking it at home, that I just want her to understand we could vary the time a little, she says she will have to think about it and check on it.

She disappears again to go "check on it." When she finally brings the antibiotic in, it's five minutes before four.

I'm wrong about her getting her nursing license from the back of a comic book. That would have taken too much intelligence to fill out the form and send it in.

On nights like this I don't know how I am going to make it through this.

At Benihana with the dinner group
from Fourth Presbyterian Church

CHAPTER 7

THE UNFORGETTABLE FIRST DATE

Since neither Jason nor I am a fan of Woody Allen, to agree to see one of his movies on our first date was our initial mistake. We only went because everyone was telling us how good this particular film was. When we got to the theater, the line was long and the theater was packed. The only two available seats still together were in the front row, a few feet from the screen. We sat with our heads goose-necked up for all one hundred and seven miserable minutes of the show. By the time it finished, I had a raging headache and I never wanted to hear the name Woody Allen again.

We'd saved dinner at the Green Door Tavern for after the movie. Throughout the show and walking over to the Tavern, I worried about having enough cash to pay for dinner. Since I'd asked Jason out, I figured I should pick up the check. But I'd run out of time and hadn't made it to an

ATM to get more money. Besides being distracted by how little cash I had in my purse, it was the coldest night Chicago had suffered in years. It was freeze-your-nostrils-shut frigid. It didn't help that I'd lost a contact the day before and had to wear my Coke-bottle glasses. Not only did they nearly freeze to my face, but every time we entered a building the thick lenses fogged up like I'd painted on a coat of gray latex. Jason was having contact troubles of his own, so he wore his glasses too which had even stouter lenses than mine. When we walked from the subzero temps outside into the Green Door Tavern—a dimly lit *warm* restaurant with table seating far in the back, way past the bar at the front—both of our spectacles immediately clouded to opaque and were useless to us. Rendered as blind as the Three Mice, we were helplessly tarrying in the entrance while waiting for our lenses to clear when the maître d' said, "Follow me," and took off somewhere into the back of the dark restaurant. There was nothing we could do but helplessly stand there by the bar. Wiping off the glasses only smeared the condensation. We simply needed a bit of time for the glass to acclimate to the heated room. The maître d' eventually swept back and snapped, "Are you coming?" That didn't help matters at all and put everything more on edge. My Woody Allen headache was only getting worse after the walk over in the twenty-below wind chill that had frozen my forehead like a block of ice. Pressed by the host to get a move on, we obeyed and stumbled our way after him into the dark, lifting and lowering our frames the whole way, hoping for even a tiny spot to clear. We finally floundered our way to the table and found our seats. With awkward, stilted conversation, we waited as we got our eyesight straightened out and were finally able to pay attention to each other again.

64

I ordered something that didn't cost too much, the whole time calculating how the total price of our order corresponded to the cash in my purse. It was the first time we shared a meal without eight other people around us, and it quickly became quite apparent that Jason was an introvert—a very *quiet* introvert. And that I was uncomfortable with silence and needed to babble stupidly to fill any void. Then to top it off, some guy, out of nowhere, came and sat down at our table with us. At first I thought Jason must have known him, but then it became clear he didn't. We exchanged some odd, uncomfortable conversation about nothing. After he got up and left, we wondered aloud if he was the manager checking to see if we liked our service and food but just forgot to explain himself. In Chicago, you never really know who the strangers are around you. At least he didn't pick the French fries off our plates. And he did help fill a few minutes of silence for us.

When dinner was over, Jason readily picked up the check and saved me the embarrassment of counting out my quarters. We returned to my building, walking through the horrid wicked cold again. When we circled through the revolving door into my lobby, of course both of our glasses fogged right back up. Being clever, I said, "'Bye again," and by the time I got my stupid glasses cleared and back on, I was standing there alone with my doorman. Jason had heard me tell him 'bye so abruptly, he took that to mean something rude like "Go away" and he just kept going around that revolving door back out into the brutal Chicago night.

Though I didn't yet know why he'd left so fast, I did have my headache, and with the whole awkward glasses thing making normal function impossible, and that weird extra guy at our table, and the stress of no money, and the horrible movie, I didn't go running after him. Not just a little bit bewildered, I took the elevator to my eleventh-floor apartment. On the way up I realized that I didn't have my keys. They were in my purse. And my purse was not on my shoulder! Somewhere in the course of the night, I'd lost it. My doorman let me use his phonebook and phone to call the Green Door Tavern, where I thought I'd had it last. They indeed found it beneath our table. (If only I'd paid the bill.) I couldn't walk back by myself—it was late and the restaurant was right by Cabrini Green. So my doorman switched on the taxi light for me outside the building's front door and I caught a cab back.

My purse was safely returned, and with my meager cash inside, I paid the cab fare. When I got inside my apartment, with a deep sigh as I kicked off my shoes and sank into my orange chenille armchair, I thought, *Oh, well. You win some—and some you don't.* Once in a while you have those kinds of dates and you simply move on. No need to sweat it. I'd just have to get through one more of the dinners and I wouldn't need to see him again. The last week of February, a group of us were going skiing in Colorado, and so I wouldn't be attending the final dinner for that month's schedule, eliminating the awkwardness that might come with being together again. Soon we could put it behind us and chalk it up to the whole silly dating scene and how not all pairings work out. Only the one more dinner to get through.

The following Tuesday at our next dinner group, I was standing with most of the gang outside the restaurant, D.B. Kaplan's, waiting for latecomers, including Jason. I was thinking about how I'd play it cool and not worry about the embarrassment of our uncomfortable evening together. I saw him approaching from a distance and prepared myself to be cool and relaxed.

But then he walked up and smiled. And I realized that my heart had taken off without telling me, thumping away in my chest like I'd just run up five flights of stairs. That lightning bolt had hit. We were going to have a second date, I would make certain of it.

CHAPTER 8

NOTES ON BEING STUNNED

Once I finally stop throwing up and my condition stabilizes a week into this nightmare, it is time to start getting better instead of worse. I need to get the fluid out of my abdomen and lungs and back into my veins where it belongs so I can get rid of it. Dr. Bengfort—the one who is my renal specialist—read an obscure study recently about a passive therapy that helps people with my problem of extreme water overload. Following the article's protocol, he has ordered my physical therapists to submerge me up to my neck in a tub of tepid, non-turbulent water twice a day for three hours total. (A soothing Jacuzzi this is not.) The tub is like a giant soup pot, a metal tank several feet tall.

Jason and I refer to this treatment as the Bengfort Effect, named after my clever nephrologist. The constant water pressure gently pushes the fluid out of my tissue and back into my circulatory system, where my recovering kidneys can work on my fluid balance and eliminate the extra water. Ever notice how when you go swimming for a while, you always have to pee, regardless of how much or little you've been drinking? That's the Bengfort Effect at work. Happens every time. If you're feeling bloated or puffy, try hanging out in a pool for a while. It will help, I promise. Before and after each of my treatments, they weigh me to monitor the benefit, and already I'm beginning to lose some of this crazy fluid—about five pounds, or two liters, of fluid each day.

Once a couple of days pass without vomiting and with me starting to feel a little more human, I get to eat again. It will be the first time food passes my lips in over a week. Food Service delivers a cup of cream of celery soup— something simple and easy to eat to test the waters, so to speak. It's probably just condensed soup with added water, from an institutional kitchen can the size of house paint. But I tell you, it is the *best soup I have ever tasted in my life*. Having no food for so long might even make eating live bugs delicious, I don't know. But I'm going to remember this most spectacular soup for the rest of my days. I'll never be able to find such a delectable dish again for*ever*.

After almost two weeks, I am finally stable enough to go home. On the day I am leaving, we ask my fertility doctor to run an early serum pregnancy test while I'm still in the hospital, a test much more sensitive than a urine stick at home. He is reluctant to at first because it is still a fraction too soon to know anything, two days earlier than we were going to run the test with the original plan before I got sick. But when he considers all we've been through, he consents and asks the nurse to order the blood test for me. But he warns us it is likely too early yet to learn anything. I know that, we know that. But after all of this, we want to try in case we actually can find out.

We are in the hallway outside of my hospital room getting ready for me to be discharged, and I look up. Walking toward us from the other end of the long corridor, my doctor is coming with a purposeful gait. When he reaches us he grins and says, "Well, the test was definitely positive."

Incredible! I am pregnant. Suddenly, the horrors of the past couple of weeks shrink into the shadows, and all I can think of is our baby who has survived this awful ordeal with us. We are going home a happy couple.

Following my release from the hospital, I am working diligently at home to keep recovering from my little brush with death. Incrementally, I regain health as I continue to deflate, losing what is left of the extra bloating and swelling in my body. Daily, my strength is improving. Jason accompanies me on brief walks to increase my endurance, the first strolls not any farther than what I did in the hospital corridors—up our few front steps and to the end of our sidewalk and back. Then we go farther, up our few front steps, to the end of our sidewalk, and down the short distance to the corner curb and straight back to the living room couch. (We live at the intersection, so in reality, it isn't very far.) Little by little, I regain strength and health. As I become stronger, my jaunts lengthen and before long, I am able to remain vertical and ambulate more like a normal person.

A couple of weeks into my home recovery, Jason gets a Tuesday off when I am beginning to noticeably turn a corner and feel better. We decide I can tolerate the ninety-minute drive to north Denver to get out of the house and visit my brother Keith's family for a dinner to celebrate our hard-won pregnancy. Before we leave town, I first need to have my usual lab test for hCG levels, the "pregnancy hormone." While I'm at the doctor's office for the blood draw, my doctor okays me to hit the road. He says it will be good for me.

In the big city with my brother and his family, we process together the whole episode of my illness and hospitalization. Then we even dare to dream. We talk about names for our future baby and speculate about what it is going to be like for us to be parents. We especially enjoy spending time with Merrie, our eighteen-month-old niece. Our own pending parenthood is truly beginning to feel real.

After our great day out of the house and having had some welcome fun and leisure, we spend the next day at home relaxing. The phone rings, and I get up off the couch to answer. I say hello, and Debbie, one of the nurses from my infertility doctor's office, is on the line. She tells me the hCG from my blood test yesterday was only 370; it hadn't gone up enough. I *hmm* and *okay* along with each thing she says, completely confused and not processing anything I hear. After we hang up, I try to relay to Jason what Debbie had said. I can't explain, because I can't digest what she'd said. I don't know what it means. I can't make sense of her words.

"What does that mean?" I ask Jason. He is as confused as I am. "I'm going to call her back. I'll ask her."

In a daze, I pick the phone back up and call her. I tell her I didn't understand what she'd said to me. She explains it all over again and adds that it means I am likely miscarrying the baby. She instructs me to stop taking the daily shots of Progesterone, which I'd been getting since the day of the embryo transfer to protect the development of a pregnancy and Jason has been injecting me with every day since I was discharged from the hospital.

Through the next two days in a confused haze, I drift along unsure what to think, unable to accept what she's told me. It doesn't feel real. On Friday, I go back in and have another hCG level drawn to see if it confirms the last one.

It rises only fifteen points. It should have doubled, tripled daily, at least. It should be going up exponentially. My doctor recommends a D&C, a dilation and curettage, worrying that if we leave things alone, an infection or other complication might occur. But I just can't agree to one, especially when my body isn't doing anything—no cramping, no bleeding. I can't believe the baby has died.

The following Monday, I have yet another blood test. This time the level doubles. My heart jumps. Is that enough? Is it okay now? My doctor assures me it doesn't mean anything, but I want to hold out and see what happens. I am not ready to give up. Particularly when the pregnancy hormone is still going up.

Another three days pass and still nothing has started to happen. I have another blood draw. This time, it has more than tripled. But my doctor says it still isn't enough of an increase to reflect a normal pregnancy. He says I am losing the baby, plain and simple. But no matter how adamantly he says it, I can't imagine having a D&C when the hCG is still rising. But he explains there is no way it can be a healthy pregnancy with the numbers creeping up so slowly. He says that even after a miscarriage, some tissue can remain that excretes the hCG, and it doesn't mean there is a viable pregnancy. But I haven't even spotted any blood, let alone "lost" the baby. Finally he shows me on ultrasound

73

that there is no embryo sac or heartbeat. At long last he convinces me. Reluctantly and sadly I agree to have the D&C the following Monday in his office.

The procedure is absolutely horrifying. Not only is my body still incredibly tender from all that has happened, but the pain meds they give me don't work. The nurse assisting the doctor keeps telling me I have to be still, but how can I possibly lie still when they are cutting the middle out of me? I can't help but cry out. They want me to be quiet, and I want me to be quiet too, but there is nothing I can do to stop it. When the doctor finally finishes, I curl up into a ball on the table and sob. He awkwardly puts his hand on my knee and states, "Ah, you're sad about losing the baby."

They've just tortured me alive. I can't think. I can't even wrap my head around the idea of the baby. No way can I do anything but sob at anyone to put an end to the agony.

He asks, "Do you want me to get Jason?"

I cry out, "*Yes!*"

Suddenly, through the blur of pain and confusion, Jason is at my side. He holds me and consoles me, not even knowing yet what has happened. He finally gets me dressed and into the car, and we go home to try to recover.

But it still isn't over. On Wednesday, a week after the D&C, when every trace of the pregnancy and its hormones should be gone, the hCG level has doubled again—though still not high enough to be a healthy pregnancy, which they make sure I understand. They are baffled but not saying much. I'm left wondering what in the world this means. Finally, they tell me I must have a tubal pregnancy. The embryo is stuck up inside my fallopian tube, destined to die there—or worse. A tubal pregnancy would explain why the D&C didn't work to clean me out and why the hormones weren't high enough in the first place. The pregnancy has always been weak and doomed. That is their working theory, anyway. What a guessing game this is. Each step, the doctors try to fit me into some profile to make sense of what they find. My body always refuses to cooperate. They have to try so many things before they finally find the right answer, if they even can.

Thursday, I go in for another ultrasound to look for the ectopic pregnancy. They can't see anything, but they can't leave things as they are. What if it *is* a tubal pregnancy and they just can't see it? It could grow large enough to erupt and I could have permanent damage, or even die. They have to figure this out. Friday, I am back in the OR for surgery. They must find the tubal pregnancy, if there is one, and remove it before it ruptures. But in the OR, they can't find anything definitive.

After I wake up from the anesthesia, they give Jason and me a few theories for what might be happening. Maybe the embryo was located close to the tube and so not completely removed with the initial D&C. Maybe I'd had twins and one was removed and one still limped along. Maybe the small uterine septum they found prevented the D&C from reaching everywhere. Who knows? But, it doesn't make everything better. Whatever the situation, they make sure this time they clean me out, cleaner than a jelly jar emptied with a rubber spatula.

A week later, I have one last follow-up hCG, and the results? It is finally zero. It is certain now. We are no longer going to have a baby.

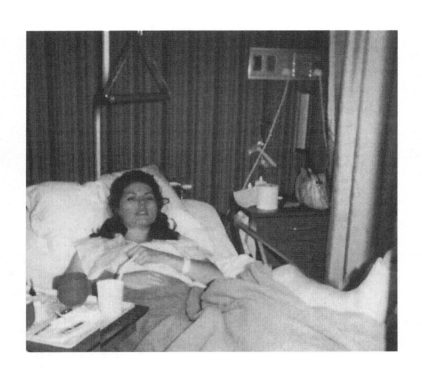

CHAPTER 9

THE BROKEN PLANS

Many of the people from the dinner group where I'd met Jason planned a week-long ski trip to Colorado, my home state. I decided to take a vacation and go too. Instead of spending money on rental skis, I wanted to put any money spent toward owning my own pair, so I'd have them for future trips. From a local sporting goods shop in Chicago, I bought skis, boots, and poles, and even had them engraved with my name. I dug out my old ski pants and jacket, secured time off from work, and on the scheduled day, bid farewell to my coworkers at the hospital, joking about seeing them after the trip if I didn't break a leg. Eleven days after my first date with Jason (who wasn't going on the trip, by the way), I boarded a plane at O'Hare, destined for Breckenridge in the mountains west of Denver.

Before leaving, I had worked the weekend, twelve-hour night shifts, plus one more graveyard shift over Monday night. After dropping by my apartment to pick up my suitcase and gear, I got on the El and headed to the airport. The entire first day was a traveling day. By the time I went to sleep that night, it was late, and I'd hardly slept for two days. The next morning our group was up and out early to hit the slopes. It was mostly sunny and a beautiful day to be in the Rockies.

At about 2:00 p.m., I was with a couple of friends from the larger group going down a blue slope, having our last run before the lifts closed for the day. I was swooshing down—left, right, left, right—having an easy-going, relaxing descent. The back and forth, back and forth, was hypnotizing, lulling me into tranquility. As I was passing to the left of a copse of trees, the mesmerizing conditions overcame me, and I nodded off.

Yes, I fell asleep skiing. That's sleep deprivation for you.

When I bolted awake, I was headed straight for the trees that forked the slope. Immediately I realized that I was going too fast to stop in time. Because my direction had changed now to the right, I pushed in that direction as hard as I could to get around the trees that were zooming toward me at full throttle.

I almost made it.

My left ski tip snagged the last tree. My leg was caught. I hit the tree mid-shin, then tumbled through the air with poles, skis, and limbs flying everywhere. When I finally slid to a stop, I lay sprawled in the snow, stunned and unmoving. Then the pain began to swell in my leg. It grew so overpowering, it took everything in my power to cope with it.

Nearby I heard the voice of my friend who'd been skiing behind me, and I screamed out to him.

"Wayne—*Wayne!*"

He appeared at my side.

"Hold my hand, hold by hand," I begged. I didn't dare move my damaged leg, but my other leg was peddling over the snow as I tried to deal with the exploding pain.

Wayne took my hand and his grip kept me anchored enough to stay relatively calm. A random man skied over and started to mess with my injured leg, apparently channeling his old Boy Scout First Aid merit badge. Wayne stopped him, telling him not to touch me, to wait until the ski patrol came. We were under the chairlift, so the skiers floating above in chairs swaying in the afternoon sun could see there'd been an accident below them. They began yelling up the line to the next chair for them to pass along a call for help.

I kept breathing, pumping my other leg across the top of the snow and squeezing the life out of Wayne's hand while we waited for help to arrive. He kept a steady stream of encouraging words coming, helping me know I could do this, I would be okay. Once the professionals came, they immobilized my leg, transferred me into a cage stretcher, and sledged me down the side of the mountain.

The doctor who treated me at the clinic told me she was sending me to a Denver suburb for surgery. She had an associate in Aurora who would take over my care and perform the operation to screw a metal plate onto my tibia, the bone that had broken. It made no sense she was sending me all the way to the eastern outskirts of Denver, adding at least another half hour to the drive. But apparently she and the Aurora doctor had a financial arrangement, so what was in my best interest wasn't the determining factor; it was her kickback for the referral. And

I didn't have the fortitude to argue. While I waited for the ambulance to come and transport me, they parked my stretcher between two other gurneys. Bookending me were two eleven-year-old boys, each having suffered a spiral fracture of his leg. With the heads of our stretchers up against the wall, we were side by side and could talk to each other.

"You're both very brave," I told them as I lay there whimpering through tears, noticing they weren't even crying.

While we waited in that hallway, each of the three of us with a splint around a broken leg, the clinic doctor dashed by and swiped a ballpoint pen up the arch of each exposed foot of our broken legs. Being very ticklish, my entire leg jerked up into a spasm, pulling at my bone fragments with the sudden, unexpected scrape. The spasm sat me straight up and, unable to even stop myself if I'd wanted to, I found my missing fortitude and yelled at the doctor

"Don't you ever do that again!"

She was checking for sensation and circulation in my foot to rule out complications after fracturing a bone. But I knew she could have simply stood at my stretcher and carefully, gently, touched my foot and examined its condition. And I told her so. She looked taken aback at my boldness, but I was having none of it. I worked with doctors, and I knew how they functioned—sometimes without thinking. It would have taken her only about fifteen seconds longer to be kind. There was no excuse for her thoughtlessness. She apologized and afterwards made sure her ballpoint pen came nowhere near either my foot or the stalwart boys' feet on either side of me.

The ambulance ride to Aurora was two-plus hours of misery. The roadway was bumpy and twisting, jarring my broken bone as we bounced our way down the mountain and then crawled through the Denver rush-hour traffic. The synthetic narcotic pain shot they'd given me left me delirious and confused but did little to alleviate my pain. And any relief it might have given me was completely gone by the time we reached Aurora.

When the EMTs finally released me into the hands of the ER staff at the hospital, it was nearly 7:00 p.m. I had to wait a while for the doctor to come to the hospital to examine me. It was a small community hospital, not a bustling teaching hospital with doctors swarming over the place like I was used to. Once my appointed doctor arrived, he was in a hurry to finish my treatment because he had dinner plans. He wondered aloud if I might be able to get by without surgery. He decided we would wait and see what happened, then he could get back to his evening plans. (That's not exactly how he phrased it, but I speak Doctor, so I knew what he meant.) Instead of an operation, he decided to just put a cast on my leg.

He called in a nurse and said to her, "Hold this here," as he raised my broken leg by only my big toe.

While my broken leg dangled in the air by my toe tightly squeezed by the nurse, the doctor wrapped my leg with casting material. He was in too much of a hurry to give me anything for pain before he started, so when he began to reduce the fracture—pushing on the bone to move it into alignment—I had no option but to scream. But that didn't seem to bother him. He kept pushing and wrapping, getting it done.

Once he finished and I was a thrashing, sweaty mess in a tangle of blankets, panting on the exam table, the nurse said meekly, "Obviously she's in a lot of pain. Can I give her something for it?"

"Yeah, okay. Give her fifty of Demerol, IM," he answered, and he walked out the door.

Afterwards, I was checked into a hospital room and admitted overnight. With the exhaustion of hardly sleeping for three days, skiing all day, plus the trauma of the whole episode, and finally the generous dose of narcotics, I was out in no time.

The next day, an x-ray showed my bone was in good alignment, so the doctor determined I wouldn't need surgery. I called my parents who lived ninety minutes away and arranged for them to come and get me once I was discharged.

With a cast the full length of my leg, from up near my groin down to my toes, I was going to have to learn to use crutches before being discharged. A physical therapist came to my hospital room to work with me, but I couldn't tolerate being up, and I started to upchuck and pass out. They had to postpone my discharge. Sadly, my grandpa and grandma came by to visit just when the PT had me out of bed and I started vomiting. Poor sweet Grandma and Grandpa. They had to see me in my horrible state. I looked as bad as Beetlejuice, and was barfing to boot.

After a lot of effort, I was finally discharged, and my parents came and swept up what was left of me and drove me to their house. The entire week was horrific. I lay on their living room sofa, my leg elevated to try to keep the swelling down. My toes kept turning purple like they were holding their breath long past what was healthful. When it was time to return to Chicago, my parents drove me back to the Denver airport, where I reunited with the rest of my traveling and skiing companions who were relishing the week they'd just spent on the slopes for a fabulous mountain vacation.

I left my shiny new monogrammed skis in my parents' garage along with the rest of my gear, so all I had was one piece of luggage. On the plane, a compassionate flight attendant gave me an entire row of seats to myself so I had a place to put my rigid full-leg cast. When the plane landed at O'Hare, it was late evening. After I waited forever at the baggage claim, ready to fall over, my bag never arrived on the conveyor belt. With some inquiry, I learned that the airline had lost my luggage. Two friends—who each got their suitcases by the way—shared a taxi with me into the city. We sat in the back seat with my cast across their laps. I appreciated the chance to spend less on transportation by sharing the fare, since I was probably out of a job and had a big credit card bill waiting for me for a vacation I didn't get.

The next day, the airlines delivered my suitcase right to my door. Turned out, it wasn't so bad they'd lost the bag. I hadn't needed to juggle it plus hobble on crutches. What a serendipitous screw-up after all. And I could sure use something serendipitous by then. The first few days back, a couple of friends brought me groceries and made sure I was doing okay, but for the most part, they didn't want to pester me too much. Plus, most of them were recovering from a long ski vacation in the beautiful Rocky Mountains and were worn out, and they were trying to get back to the ol' grind themselves.

That gave me a lot of quiet time.

I called my supervisor at work and told her I'd broken my leg. She thought I was joking, since that was the last thing we'd talked about as I left the NICU on my way to O'Hare. But once she realized it was true, she arranged for me to work as the desk clerk as soon as I was able so I wouldn't have to go without pay. They even paid me my regular RN wage, instead of what the desk clerks made. She was a gem.

The day after I got home, I received a large manila envelope in the mail from Mr. Jason with a copy of *GQ* and *Vanity Fair* and another magazine article he'd Xeroxed for me. I was amazed how quickly he'd heard about my accident and responded with reading material for me. But after getting the package, I didn't hear from him for a while. I began to feel like maybe I'd imagined the chemistry between us. When he finally did call to stop by, he said he'd figured I'd been flooded with visits from all the other friends and didn't want to intrude. I assured him there had been no flood.

Several times he came over after he got off work, bringing a deck of cards. He sat with me for hours playing gin rummy. He also told me he'd mailed the magazines before he even knew I'd broken my leg. He simply wanted to share some of his favorite reads with me.

Apparently, I wasn't wrong about the chemistry.

Once I'd recovered enough to get out and about, he asked me out for our second date. We went to the Art Institute and then dinner at Gino's Pizza on North LaSalle. At the Art Institute he arranged for a wheelchair from the museum's checkroom so I wouldn't have to crutch around the enormous place. He rolled me from one artwork to another, impressing me with his knowledge of the fine arts, gained from a class on art appreciation he'd taken in college. We saw Grant Wood and Edward Hopper, among others, and he told me their history and significance. I was thoroughly impressed.

After I started getting around more on crutches, we hoofed it around the city together to increase my stamina. Jason would point out a bench a few blocks away on a corner and encourage me to make that bench my goal, where I'd get to sit and rest as a reward once I got there. He helped me gain the strength and mobility that I needed to be independent and get by on my own when required.

Easter came, and I hoped we would be able to do something special together. But Jason had some previous commitment and wasn't available. On Easter morning, I put on one of my high-heeled pumps and crutched my way across the five blocks to get from my apartment on Chicago and Dearborn to Fourth Presbyterian Church across from the Hancock Building. I was going to my friend Mary's for Easter dinner after church. When the service finished, she went to get her car to give me a ride while I waited at the curb, leaning on my crutches outside the church on East Delaware.

Standing there, I glanced down the sidewalk at another church exit and saw Jason walking out with a group of people, all of them wearing their best Easter outfits and happy smiles. Oh, the wonderful time they were having. Laughing, fellowshipping. A woman I didn't know sidled up next to Jason and slipped her hand into the crook of his elbow, and the four jovial couples walked the other direction, on their way—no doubt—to a fabulous Easter brunch in a luxurious restaurant.

I felt gut punched. My throat tightened, and my eyes flooded with tears. Mary drove up and hopped out to open the door for me and help with my crutches. I quickly sucked up the emotion as best as I could and concentrated on getting my awkward self into the car without making a blubbering scene.

Easter dinner was hard to get through, and I was subdued, trying not to let the disappointment leak out, which I knew was likely to, in embarrassing ways, if I were to attempt to open my mouth to speak. I let Mary and her other guests do the talking and did little myself to add to the conversation. I couldn't wait to get home and have a good cry alone.

The week progressed while I moped, stuck at home, sitting in my orange armchair with my cast and swelling foot propped up next to the sliding glass door to my tiny triangular balcony. The view was southwest, and I could pine while gazing at Sears Tower or by watching ridiculous daytime TV on my tiny black and white. I couldn't help but rerun the scene in my mind of that woman taking Jason's arm like she owned it, walking by his side, smiling up at him. I'd misunderstood so much, apparently.

But then Jason called to arrange a visit. Of course I agreed. I still wanted him as a friend.

When he came to visit, I got brave and told him I saw the group with his friends, and that I saw he had a date on his arm. Without hesitation, he assured me the Easter party was put on the calendar before our first date. And the girl I'd seen take his arm? She'd had her sights set on him for a while as a beau for herself, but she was taking liberties—the feelings weren't mutual. He liked *me*.

On our third date, we went to a jazz club in the Loop for dinner where we heard the pianist Bobby Enriquez.

And that was the final "real" date we had. At least the kind where one of us called up the other and officially asked the other out. By the third date, we knew the chemistry was real. After that, we started doing everything together.

CHAPTER 10

NOTES ON BEING DETERMINED

I am sitting at the computer in our second bedroom—the room that would have been our baby's nursery—and a tsunami of grief blindsides me, leaving me sobbing over my keyboard.

Though the grief is real, in the midst of the sorrow the strangest sensation swoops in alongside my heartache. Or more accurately, beneath my heartache. I feel as though my spirit is levitating, held up by a greater power—like giant, loving hands cradling my heart, which keep me from scraping the rugged surface of wherever my emotions would plummet, where I'd shatter into more painful fragments. As I cry, I have an amazing sense that a caring being holds me, comforting me in the loss, somehow soothing the worst of the pain, maybe even anesthetizing the most extreme agony of the loss.

Jason hears me from the other room and comes in. He takes me in his arms and holds me, quietly, letting me weep and grieve, allowing the process of healing to begin.

During my leave of absence from work as a maternal-child homecare nurse for high-risk moms-to-be, sick neonates, and pediatric patients, I concentrate on recuperating, grieving, and processing all that has happened. I realize that I don't want to spend every day taking care of pregnant ladies and newborn babies, so I submit my resignation. Once I recover, I will look into a job that won't be a constant reminder of how I've so miserably failed to have a baby.

Six weeks pass, and the time has come to return to the doctor's office to make a plan. In order to keep my endometriosis from growing back and causing more internal damage and scarring, my doctor wants me to go back on Lupron, the drug that would induce premature menopause and keep everything in check. I don't want to be on medication that will make it impossible for me to get pregnant. I'm not yet ready to completely put away the idea of having our own baby. We don't know what we are going to do. Only as we talk it over standing in the kitchen when it is time to leave for the appointment do Jason and I decide to ask the doctor if we can try the ZIFT one more time. And if it doesn't work, we will give up on the idea of having our own biological child. Maybe in time we can adopt. Or maybe just enjoy being a couple. We really like each other, so that could be okay.

At the appointment when we tell the doctor what we are thinking, his mouth opens and his jaw hangs loose from the shock of hearing us say what we want to do. He can't believe that after all we have been through, we are ready so soon to try again.

But I'm thinking, what's a little extra fluid? We gals usually get a little bloaty every month anyway. Hey, I am resilient. I'm young. We explore the possibility together, and he agrees we can do it again with reduced amounts of medication and closer monitoring. Being extra careful, he believes that we will be able to avoid the extreme complications of the first attempt. Even before we leave his office, his nurse gives me a pill and little paper cup of water, and I begin my oral medication to prepare for the injections.

By the middle of June, Jason is giving me two shots everyday. Neither of us likes that part of the process. To cope with the needles and to attempt to stay relaxed, as I lie on my stomach on the bed waiting for the shot, I sing old TV sitcom theme songs while he gets the syringe ready. It's an effective distraction to try to access those old archives in my brain. While I concentrate on remembering the song lyrics, he swoops in and gets the needle business done.

Just sit right back and you'll hear a tale, a tale of a—Yow!

Come and listen to a story 'bout a man named Jed, a poor mountaineer—Ouch!

With frequent blood work and ultrasounds, the doctor makes sure my body is tolerating the medications well enough and not going out of whack like last time. If for a second the results even hint that I am going to go into the danger zone, we'll have to abort the whole effort and stop everything. But my levels and response to the meds remain within acceptable limits, and we are given the go-ahead to move to the next level. On a very precisely determined Sunday morning, our alarm clock starts beeping at 2:30 a.m., and we stagger out of bed. It is time for Jason to give me the final shot that will prepare the eggs—exactly thirty-five hours before I am scheduled to go into surgery again for egg retrieval.

On Tuesday afternoon, the anesthesiologist puts the mask over my face, pushes the sedative into my IV, and I go to sleep. During my dreamless, drug-induced nap, they obtain eighteen eggs—five fewer than the first time. When they mix the eggs with the sperm, ten of them fertilize. By the second day eight are alive, dividing and growing in their Petri dish. Eight is the same number we had going into the first ZIFT procedure. Though the doctor and surgical facility didn't have cryopreservation then and we couldn't freeze any, they've since added the capability to store embryos so we don't have to use them all at once. It is an incredibly difficult decision to decide how many to use since the last time we put in eight embryos and still lost them all. So with the doctor's guidance, we decide to have five transferred and three frozen. It is good that this second time we have options, and we are confident we've made a good plan.

But as I am being wheeled into the OR, the microbiologist rushes to the side of my stretcher and says the three designated for freezing aren't in good enough condition to store after all. Each embryo is graded and the grade has to be a certain quality to warrant freezing. We can't swap them out for the best ones, because those need to go into me for the greatest chance of success.

We have to decide right there in that minute what to do. The OR staff is waiting. My procedure has its allotted time on the facility schedule. We must keep things rolling. There is no time to think it over or sleep on it. Jason and I look at each other. We know we aren't going to throw them away. Rather than discard anybody, we choose to have them all transferred.

"Use 'em all. Put them all in," I answer.

After the surgery (as before, they transferred the embryos via a mini-laparotomy—a two-inch incision in my abdomen), we go home for me to rest, recuperate, and hopefully become pregnant. My oldest sister, Cyndi, calls to see what I am doing.

Lying on the couch trying to be motionless and positive, I answer optimistically, "Implanting, I hope."

During the next week Jason continues to give me progesterone shots each day. By now, I've had nearly one hundred intramuscular injections. (Those are the kind with the long needles that sink deeply into a muscle.) I've grown too familiar with the words to *Gilligan's Island* and *The Beverly Hillbillies* and have to start using theme songs less familiar to me. *Keep Manhattan, just give me that … um … Ow!* As long as I am stuck on a word when the needle goes in, I don't notice it quite so much.

By the eighth day after the embryo transfer, I have gained only four pounds. Though I'm constantly worried the vomiting is going to suddenly come on because of how abruptly it started last time, it hasn't happened. Not yet. Things are looking okay.

But by the ninth day, nausea hits me like a runaway shopping cart. The nausea grows until I have trouble getting out of bed on the tenth day. Two days later, I realize that I feel very different from the last go-round (that is, how I felt once I wasn't dying anymore). Just for kicks, I want to try a home pregnancy test. It's two days before a laboratory blood test is supposed to be sensitive enough to detect the hCG hormone, but the suspense is pretty intense and I want to know if there is any chance it might have worked this time. I have to do it first thing in the morning because the hormone needs all night to concentrate in my sample.

And bingo. The stick is clearly positive.

Even with my nausea, we go out to dinner to celebrate. I don't eat much but I am intensely happy, flying high. When I have my blood drawn the next day, the results are confirmed. I have a strong pregnancy with a good hCG level. We schedule an ultrasound for two weeks away when the embryo will be visible enough to see a heartbeat and sac, when our little tadpole can be evaluated for the first time.

The next weekend, we have tickets to go to the mountain town of Central City with my parents and Cyndi to see one of my favorite operas, Gounod's *Faust*, at the city's historic opera house. My dad is playing in the pit. For many years of my youth, my dad played violin in the pit orchestra for their summer opera seasons. Sometimes we went up to see him and stayed in a cabin or visited just for the day, fishing for trout in the cold mountain river with him between his performances. While he stood out in the middle of the roaring water wearing thigh-high waders, casting again and again and often slipping a shiny, writhing trout into the wicker creel hanging from his shoulder, my three siblings and I stood on the bank holding over the shallow pools our impromptu poles made of pine sticks with fishing line tied to the ends, our hooks baited with orange salmon eggs. I don't remember that we kids ever caught anything that way, but my dad caught enough fish for us all. He taught me on his catch how to kill and gut a trout for dinner right there at the riverside.

When Jason and I had ordered our tickets for *Faust* several weeks ago, I was eager to return to the quaint town I remembered so well from childhood. Now, knowing only for five days that I've become pregnant, I still want to go in spite of being weak, nauseated, and a bit shaky. No one but Cyndi knows I'm pregnant. We don't want to broadcast anything too soon after what happened before. But she had gone with me when Jason couldn't for a procedure and knew what we were attempting again. So once we get to Central City, she helps set a gentle pace as we trek the steep hills around town and climb the stairs of the opera house to sit up in the balcony. *Bravo!* The performance is fantastic.

When I was little and had visited the town, it wasn't yet a casino hub like it is today. But the year before our visit, gambling was legalized and several casinos opened. Cyndi brought along a roll of nickels for each of us so we can take a shot at changing our fortunes.

Well, none of our fortunes is altered, but we have fun dropping in the coins and watching the spinning reels blur around before they slow down and almost match up. We win a few nickels back, but not enough to cover the cost of a cup of coffee. Regardless, the entire trip is a wonderful, much-needed outing on a beautiful summer day.

The following week, I decide to go to a maternity shop and buy one outfit. At least one time, I want to do something pregnant women do while I am still pregnant and consider myself a mom to the baby growing inside of me. At the checkout, the cashier recognizes that I am a new mom-to-be and asks all the nice questions to give me a chance to gush about being "on the nest." I tell her it might even be twins because I am so nauseated and my hormones are so high. I'm sure she hears that all the time. Newly pregnant women often speculate about what extreme circumstances they might have because their mothers-in-law tell them they're so much bigger than usual or twins run in the family on Grandma's great uncle's side. I make certain to relish the entire outing because I know it may not last, and I want to savor every minute and aspect of being pregnant while I can. For now, no matter what is to come, I am pregnant. There is a baby inside of me. I am a mom.

CHAPTER 11

THE BOAT PARTY

Jana—a jovial friend who always kept me in rollicking laughter—and I were both invited in September of '85 to a party. The location of the soiree was unique and intriguing; the party was to take place on a riverboat that would transport us along the Chicago River, then out onto Lake Michigan. Our mutual friend, Mark, was hosting the party with three of his guy friends, each of whom could invite twelve guests, the total of which would fill the capacity of the boat. Jana and I were two of Mark's allotted dozen.

In spite of the extraordinary circumstances of the party venue, I didn't want to go. Jana tried to coax me. She didn't want to go alone. I didn't want to go at all. But she kept asking.

Finally I said, kind of throwing it out to the universe, "Okay, I'll go, but only if I meet my Prince Charming there, the Man of My Dreams, the one who I'll marry so I'll not have to date anyone else ever again."

I thought the excessive stipulation would get me off the hook.

Jana said, "Okay, I'm sure something can be worked out. Go get changed. You're coming."

It felt like she wasn't taking the negotiations as seriously as I would have liked.

Later, in our party dresses and dolled up for the evening, we walked down the dock and waited on the gangplank to embark. Mark greeted Jana and me, welcoming each of us with a proffered long-stemmed red rose. It turned out—poor guy—his girlfriend and future wife (they didn't know that yet) had gotten stuck on a business trip out of town so not only would she miss the party, but he couldn't give her the dozen roses he'd already purchased for her. So Jana and I and the other nine of Mark's guests each got a stem as we arrived.

We accepted our roses, boarded, and I immediately looked around, scoping out the crowd. "Okay," I said *sotto voce* to Jana, "where is he? Where is that guy I'm going to marry?"

She laughed and said, "Let's go get some wine and find some people we know."

I said, "No, really. Jana, I meant that. Part of the deal of coming with you."

Her jolly, full laughter filled the humid air, but then she let the subject drop. "Where's the wine do you suppose?"

See? She wasn't taking it seriously.

As soon as all the expected party guests were aboard, we cast off from the pier and trawled the river for a time. Then we transferred through the locks to prepare to navigate out onto Lake Michigan. In spite of myself, I loved it. It was unexpectedly thrilling. I was like a child enthralled by the scene, leaning over the railing to take in everything around me. In the locks, the gates closed, and the water level rose over several minutes. I'd never seen the process before and it fascinated me. Once the gates opened, we proceeded out onto the lake. As the sun set, the view was breathtaking. After it was dark, the water glistened with thousands—maybe millions—of shimmering miniature moons while the twinkling Chicago skyline mirrored itself in the black water along the shoreline.

Throughout the evening, Jana and I mingled, talked, and laughed, and we met several new people. At one point, I left Jana to explore the boat and ventured down to the lower deck to find the tables spread with party food and drinks. Among other delectables, there were some fantastic brownies. Gooey, chewy, rich and delicious. (I've always been a sucker for a good chocolate brownie.) I hung out with the brownies for a while, visiting with other brownie enthusiasts, including a guy and his date serving them (or maybe pretending to serve them so they could keep testing them). After getting my fill (if that's even possible) of the superb brownies and having communed with my fellow chocolate lovers, I went back up top to enjoy the night breeze and the sights and sounds of the water voyage before we headed back to port when the evening came to its conclusion.

When it was over and we disembarked, Jana said, "See? Not so bad."

She was right. It had been incredible. I was so glad I'd gone. Even though the terms of my negotiations didn't come to fruition, the experience was amazingly memorable. I was deeply grateful that Jana had made me go.

It was such an astounding memory for me that after Jason and I had been together for a while, I was telling him about the unbelievable party I'd gone to the previous year. I described the entire event in minute detail—the docks, the boat, the locks, the roses, the glimmering water and lights. I told him about the party and the food—especially the brownies—and the people, so friendly and fun. And how incomparably, nearly indescribably cool the lake is at night in the moonlight on a boat in late summer in view of the shore and the Chicago skyline. I went on and on. It was important to me that he understand and appreciate what a wondrous experience it had been for me. That absolutely fantastic boat trip was a little life-changing for me, and I wanted to share it with him.

Then I told him more about Mark, because I'd since gotten to know Mark better and met more of his friends. The circumstances of the gathering, I'd come to learn, was that he'd thrown the boat party with buddies of his with whom he'd gone to Mexico, a close group of bachelors who did all kinds of things together. I said I knew one of the other guys, Bob, who happened to be a man Jason knew. And Chip, another of Mark's friends whom I'd met. There was one other man I didn't know, but he was the fourth guy who'd rented the boat with Mark, Bob, and Chip.

Jason liked my story and how enthusiastic I was about it. He smiled and nodded the whole while that I chattered on. His response encouraged me to elaborate more and more, which I was happy to do since it was truly a highlight of my experiences in Chicago up to that point. His nonverbal cues kept me talking. He was clearly interested and maybe even fascinated by my story. Finally he chuckled.

"What? Why are you laughing?" I asked.

He paused, watching me closely. Then finally he said—with an even bigger smile, "It was me. I was the fourth guy. That was *my* boat party. And I was the brownie guy."

Whoa! Wait. My mind was blowing. "You?" I summoned to my mind the memory of the couple sitting at the table with the brownies. The guy was only a vague outline of a man, without any details, a gray face blob with hair. Except I could remember he had his arm around the girl sitting next to him in the booth seat. What she looked like, I had no recollection. I guess I'd spent more time making eye contact with the brownies than the handsome face guarding the brownies.

"You're kidding! That was you?"

He nodded. "Yep. Bob, Chip, Mark, and I went to Ixtapa, Mexico last year. We rented the boat and hosted the party together."

Inconceivable. Jana, or the universe, or *somebody*, had come through. The stipulations of my negotiations had in fact been actualized. I'd met my Prince Charming that night after all!

CHAPTER 12

NOTES ON BEING HAPPILY NAUSEATED

Happily, I am battling nausea. I am so content to be pregnant and staying that way, I don't mind these consequences, even if it means lying around doing practically nothing but nibbling saltines and sipping ginger ale. While I'm idling along, the phone jingles, and the nurse supervisor from the NICU at the city hospital is on the line and offers yours truly a new job as a NICU staff nurse. During the time between my two pregnancies, I'd applied for a job to help make ends meet and hopefully recover from giving the doctor our entire nest egg. And to buy groceries. And pay for insurance. And to keep the lights on. I'd filled out the application before we'd even thought about trying our second round of ZIFT. My interview was one week after my home pregnancy test. I thought I'd better start pulling my weight around here and help bring home some of the bacon. This job is quite good news. I'll be very happy to get back into hospital acute care nursing. My start date for hospital orientation, which will last a couple of weeks before I'm assigned patients, is in three days, Monday, July 27.

Until then, today—Friday—I have my ultrasound scheduled to take a look at our little peanut. Jason can't get off time from work—an awful hourly minimum-wage job making phone calls to convince people to switch long-distance phone carriers—so I have to go alone.

As the doctor performs the ultrasound and studies the screen on the monitor, I'm lying on the exam table nervously prattling on and on about all the possibilities—including the chance of twins, considering how high my hCG is and how nauseated I've been. Two babies would be okay with me actually, since it has cost so much to just get pregnant. It would be nice to get a BOGO deal.

I finally stop my nonstop blathering when I notice the doctor has grown remarkably still and silent, his eyes glued to the ultrasound screen.

"What? Do you see more than one?" I excitedly ask.

After a pause, he says, "Do you have a calculator?"

I scream.

After I catch enough air to breathe again, I finally manage to squeak out, "What do you mean?"

"Hang on. Just give me a minute here. I'm still looking."

While trying not to hyperventilate, I am impatient and keep pestering him for an immediate explanation.

He swivels the monitor toward me so I can see what he's been examining so intently. I hold my breath. I stop blinking and stare. I think my heart even stops beating for a few seconds while I brace myself to see what in the world is on that screen, what is inside of my body.

He points with his pen, clicking the tip against the glass of the monitor. He counts. "One...two...three. See here?" He circles a spot on the grainy image with the nib of the ballpoint. "I found another sac here but I can't find a heartbeat. It might have implanted and then petered out. Let me look a little longer."

While he continues to study the screen, I find my voice again and begin to jabber incessantly, 100 miles per hour, tittering about triplets and what that could possibly mean. My mind is flipping out. This is more than I truly considered, even if I'd joked about it. Is this real? Am I dreaming? This can't be happening!

He rotates the monitor toward me once again and says, "Here," clinking his pen against the glass over the fourth bubble. A tiny white smudge is rapidly fluttering at the edge of a larger gray blur, identical to the other three bubbles.

My giddy chatter disappears, sucked out of my throat in a sudden vacuum. My every blink is slow, arduous. Utter disbelief eclipses my brain. I can't process this. Shock. I'm going into shock. My mind can't grasp this. What does he mean? Four? *Four babies?* I throw my hands over my face and shake my head from side to side. Incomprehensible. The only words I can get out I murmur, muffled, into my palms, where I'm hiding. "I can't have four babies."

"I know," he says gently. He pats me on the shoulder. "Get dressed and come into my office. We'll talk."

He walks out and closes the door, leaving me alone in the small room. My mind is racing, trying to put together cohesive thoughts. My heart pounds against the inside of my ribcage. I slip off the exam table and pull on my clothes. I don't even notice what I'm doing. My shirt could be inside-out and upside-down and I wouldn't know. I open the door and peer into the empty hallway, then find my way to his office where he is waiting for me, his cowboy boots propped up on the edge of his giant oak desk. When I walk in, he drops his feet back to the carpet and leans forward on his elbows. I sink into the chair across from him.

He gets right to the point. "Selective reduction. I don't do it here, but you can go to Denver."

Using ultrasound for visualization, they'd put a needle through my abdominal wall, insert the needle into the hearts of two of the fetuses—whichever are easiest to reach—and inject potassium. The drug would stop their hearts. They'd die, reabsorb, and I'd then try to successfully carry a twin pregnancy to term. That is, if doing the procedure doesn't cause me to miscarry the entire pregnancy.

Before having any of the high-tech procedures to get pregnant, my doctor had talked to me about the possibility of conceiving many babies, and I'd sort of thought, yeah, yeah, yeah. I'm sure that won't happen to me.

He'd said, "Let's say that after a shipwreck there's a lifeboat floating in the ocean and there are five or six survivors in the boat. Now, there are only enough supplies for two of the castaways. Everyone knows that if they all try to survive, all of them will die. But, if they throw three or four people overboard, then the odds to live will go up so high for the two left, it's worth choosing to toss some overboard."

The day he'd told me that, I was simply trying to survive getting pregnant and hoping to have a baby. One baby. I have been taking each step as it comes, not crossing any bridge until I am actually standing right on the very edge of it. I hardly believed I'd get pregnant, let alone face getting so incredibly pregnant.

The very moment he said there are four heartbeats (at least as soon as I stopped screaming), my maternal instincts flew into high gear, and I became suddenly protective like I didn't know was possible. I'd seen my four little babies inside me, only six weeks old, working against all odds to keep their little hearts beating. How, after all we'd gone through to give any of them the chance to live, would I take that away from them? I am not about to even consider throwing a single one of them overboard.

I know there are absolutely no guarantees, that odds are against us, that we will probably have trouble, that maybe they will all die, or maybe have terrible problems. But I also know, whatever happens I want to, I must, give them all the best chance to live that I possibly can.

Right there in the room as I am processing everything, God—or who I can only assume must be God, because it's been so long since we were on speaking terms—whispers into my soul. He says to me that every step of the way, he will be with us. We won't have to do this alone.

I tell my doctor immediately that that's not what I want to do. I'm not interested. He encourages me to think about it, to consider the risks. I reiterate my decision. He wants me to go home and talk to Jason about it.

"No. We're not going to do it."

"Well," he says, putting his boots back up to rest on the edge of his desk, "if you do decide to go through with this, if anyone can do it, it is you, Cheri."

I leave in a daze—shocked, excited, overwhelmed, and trying hard to wrap my brain around this new reality. It is time to go tell Jason the news, that he is looking at the possibility of becoming the father to lots of babies all at once. He is about to get off work so I don't have to explode with anticipation for too long. He walked to work this morning so I could have the car to go to my appointment. I drive over, then perch on the bench in front of the entryway into his building. I sit there grinning from ear to ear, smiling and nodding to a lot of strangers walking in and out of the door, trying not to jump out of my skin while I wait for Jason to appear.

Finally, he is strolling out the double glass door entrance. I jump up to meet him. My smile is contagious, or he doesn't know what to think of me so he smiles back, and smiles some more, nodding, like *So…?* and I stare at him, until he finally says, "Well…?"

I can't even speak. I hold up four fingers and mouth the number.

"Four? Four. *Four?*" he stammers. He plops down on the bench. I sit next to him.

We stay there side by side a long time—stunned, smiling, shaking our heads and laughing out loud at each other. But there are no words. We are both speechless. Literally speechless. Utterly, totally unable to speak. This one tops everything else we've ever experienced. We are pregnant with quadruplets.

CHAPTER 13

THE ENGAGEMENT

In August of 1986, I went home with Jason to Minnesota as his plus-one for his sister's wedding. I met his dad, Jack, and his two siblings and stepmom. (His mom had passed away suddenly in the summer before his senior year of high school.) This same weekend, his brother brought home his new fiancée as well for everyone to meet for the first time. (Their wedding would be two weeks later.) At the reception for his sister's wedding, Jason and I danced together and gave all the aunts and cousins plenty to whisper and speculate about. "Jay" had never brought home a girl before. Especially a big-city girl who was daring enough to wear a hat to the wedding like she thought she was British or something. By the end of the weekend, they concluded that this one looked like she might be a keeper, someone special, and it gave the small-town folk plenty to talk about.

At Christmastime four months later, Jason went home with me to Colorado and met my family.

Almost three months later, on Saturday, March 14, 1987, a little more than a year after that awful Woody Allen movie and wickedly cold night of miscommunication, we were together enjoying my weekend off from work. (I worked at the hospital every other weekend.) The two of us were sitting in Jason's one room studio apartment above the Chicago Italian restaurant, Salvatore's. We were finishing up a meal when our conversation turned to our future. My apartment was two blocks away and like Jason, I had about six months left on my lease.

Not sure exactly how to say it, I brought up that we'd each need to decide before long and tell our landlords if we were going to renew our leases for another year. I asked him what he thought about that, if he thought we were going to do anything that would impact our plans, like make things permanent between us. Would we get married and move to one place or would we keep our separate apartments?

He thought a moment and indicated with a slight nod that maybe he was thinking we should go ahead with the idea and move into one apartment.

To make sure I understood him correctly, I asked, "So does that mean we're engaged?"

He smiled and clearly nodded this time. "I guess so," he said.

The next Wednesday he took me down to Jewelers Row in the Loop to look for a ring. We met Rumi Engineer, a plump, jolly jeweler who had a shop on Wabash Avenue, one store among many in the jewelers mall below the elevated subway platform over the street. Rumi Engineer was gregarious and told a lot of stories. Like when his grandfather came over from India and crossed through

Ellis Island. He needed to choose an Americanized name for his family, so he picked Engineer for their new surname. As Rumi was sharing his family history, he poured out a stream of glistening diamonds from a black velvet drawstring bag onto a velvet pad on his lighted glass case. Then he let us use his loupe to look closely at the miniature river of costly rocks while he taught us about carats and points, clarity and color grades, flaws and facets, and how to pick a good diamond.

With his expert help, we found the diamond we liked—a brilliant round-cut jewel. After that, he introduced us to his collection of ring settings by flourishing slotted velvet trays with rows of shiny bands made of gold or platinum. All the engagement rings had empty prongs, each like a tiny hand with its fingers spread open, waiting to take hold of a new sparkling stone. Even with his trays of many possibilities, we didn't find the setting that met my hopes. He told us he'd get another shipment soon, that there were always different styles coming in. When we returned another day to see his new choices, we found what we were looking for—a swirled gold wedding band with nine channel-cut diamonds. The gold band spooned along the curve of the matching engagement ring which had three channel-cut diamonds on either side of the 6-prong setting where Rumi would mount our chosen gem.

Once we decided on my rings, we began looking for a wedding venue. Our leases were up after September so we were aiming for an autumn wedding, which was only six months away. That didn't leave much time, as wedding planning goes. All the places we checked were booked solid for Saturday weddings throughout the fall and into winter. We'd have to get married on a different day of the weekend if we didn't want to delay until the next year. We thought long and hard about having an intimate wedding on one of the boats like the one where we'd met—it would weigh anchor on the Chicago River, then move onto Lake Michigan; we'd have a string quartet play Mozart on the deck and hors d'oeuvres served by hired caterers after we exchanged vows—but since the season would already be changing, we realized it would probably be too cold, plus it would drastically reduce the number of guests we could have. We let prudence win and decided against the boat wedding. Many times since then, I've wished we'd ignored what Prudence told us and had our wedding on the water. But of course, that's after having the most beautiful wedding I could have imagined, so maybe since I'd experienced the one, it was easier to wish for the other too.

Jason was a head usher at Fourth Presbyterian Church on Michigan Avenue, which sits across the street from the Hancock Building. The church, built in 1914, is a famous landmark listed on the National Register of Historic Places. Being a Sunday Morning Usher at Fourth Pres was a prestigious and prized position, with many requirements to fulfill the office accordingly therein. The male ushers wore dark blazers, formal morning suit striped trousers, and ties in muted tones. The scarce women of the group wore dark conservative dresses or suits. A few select scripted greetings were pre-ordained that were to keep unruly chit chat in check. Absolutely no raised voices would be brooked to announce available seating. The contingent was not to lift any arm above the waist, and they used silent hand signals discretely at their hips to indicate to each other any open seats or closed pews. (Until two minutes before the service commenced, they held certain pews for latecomers that were owned by families whose ancestors had tithed enough in bygone years to still control that sanctuary real estate.)

The best part of all this? Because he was a member of the church in good standing, he was eligible to have his wedding there. And it just happened that it was available on a Friday evening the first weekend in October. We snatched up the time and made the reservation. We had our date. We'd be married on October 2 at 5:00 p.m.

The Streeterville Holiday Inn (more recently the DoubleTree Hotel), was on Ohio Street near the Chicago River—only two blocks east of Michigan Avenue and two blocks west of Lake Michigan. The hotel offered an unbelievable deal for a reception. They would provide a buffet dinner with choice of fish, chicken, or roast beef; six salads; green beans almondine; potatoes au gratin; chocolate and vanilla mousse; white wine for everyone, plus an open bar—for only $25 per person. They also threw in a free night's stay for the bride and groom in the hotel's honeymoon suite—nearly a $700 value, they eagerly told us.

In April, I needed to make a trip to Colorado. While I was there, a good friend threw me a bridal shower. I also went shopping for a wedding dress with my mom. We shopped at the Gray Rose, an exclusive high-end fashion house that opened in 1938. One dress I tried on cost $500 and it was my mom's favorite. A different one was actually my favorite but it cost $200 more. My mom's choice won because I couldn't afford spending the additional money. The one I bought fit me perfectly except for the length. Since I wouldn't be in Colorado again before the wedding to do future fittings, the dress flew home with me in a white zipped garment bag. I did the adjustments myself. I also made my veil, covering a teardrop hat form with satin, beads, and sequins. On the little cap I attached my sister Suzy's wedding veil—tulle that she and I had hand-sewn countless beads, sequins, and lace appliqués on for her wedding four years before.

Several of my hospital coworkers had recently married so everyone had helpful suggestions for jewelers, photographers, and bakers. The church wouldn't allow a videographer to film unless they stood out of sight, way over on one side behind the pulpit, so we decided to forego video. Why pay $150 for a thirty minute video of the back of a stone pillar? I ordered a gold wedding band for Jason and had it engraved inside, "CAR to JPG 10-2-87" (Cheri Ann Robinson to Jason Pierce Gillard, and the wedding date). Cyndi wanted to arrange the flowers, and I loved the idea. I chose white roses and alstroemeria and ordered them from a local florist shop, plus the greenery and materials she'd need to arrange them. I also found clear glass oil lamps with hurricane cylinders to go in the center of each bouquet.

Music was especially important to me for the entire affair. For the ceremony, we arranged to use Fourth Pres's historic pipe organ and the church organist, an esteemed musician. For the prayer and meditation, I asked my dad and Cyndi—both career violinists—to play the second movement of the "Bach Double," the most breathtaking violin duet I've ever heard. We hired a local symphony trumpeter to perform Mouret's *Rondeau* with the organ for our fanfare recessional.

For the reception, I adamantly wanted a string quartet but couldn't afford the cost of a professional ensemble, so I called the music departments of universities around Chicago and connected with some music majors at DeVry who had their own string quartet. I went to hear the students at one of their gigs and loved their quality. They were half the price of local professionals. It was an easy decision. We checked dates and they were available for the reception. It was coming together beautifully.

CHAPTER 14

NOTES ON BEING PREGNANT

Jason and I spend the weekend trying to *start* to get used to the idea that we've made four babies together, and they're currently living inside of me. Besides the mental processing, all I do otherwise is battle nausea, mostly lying around on the couch. And though I've not gotten any whopping case of ovarian hyperstimulation syndrome this time, I still have mild symptoms that physically compromise me. Plus, I am still recovering from abdominal surgery. In spite of this new strange reality that I might eventually give birth to somewhere between one to four babies, plus feeling weak and achy, I start my new job as planned on the Monday after my Friday ultrasound.

With a dozen or more other new hospital hires who are also beginning orientation, I'm sitting in a classroom full of school desks, my sweating can of 7-Up and a plastic baggie of saltine crackers on my Formica desktop. I'm trying not to puke as the head of security gives a lecture about how well his staff works to keep the hospital employees safe. (This is the same place they found a dead guy in the stairwell not too long before this orientation, according to the local paper. The head of security doesn't mention this detail.) Finally, after persevering without throwing up through several more presentations from different department heads, they give us a lunch break, and I dash to the bathroom.

And I discover I am bleeding.

Oh, no. No, no! Not again!

My friend Lisa who works in Human Resources happens to come into the bathroom while I'm in there. As soon as I see her, my fears, my crashing hopes, tumble out. Grabbing onto her arm, I barrage her with my dread and anxiety. Sympathetic and gentle, she leads me to her office and lets me use her phone to call my doctor. With my heart pounding, I dial his office. He is out of town again. He's vacationing in Hong Kong this time, on our nest egg no doubt. So I put a call into the doctor covering for him. He isn't readily available either. Probably out on lunch break too. But at least that's closer than China. I lie on Lisa's office couch waiting for what seems like an eternity, my mind whirling with the probability that I'm miscarrying again, trying to brace myself to face the disappointment one more time. When the on-call doctor finally answers my page, he tells me to go home and lie down.

This leaves me feeling so helpless. But there is little to do for it. Just rest. But come to think of it, I am, in fact, quite practiced up on that lately, aren't I? This is something

I can do. So I get myself home and rest as well as I possibly can. I lie down and barely move for the next few days. And you know what? It seems to help. The bleeding mostly stops. When my doctor returns and I see him, he explains that bleeding with higher multiples is more common than with single pregnancies. It doesn't *necessarily* mean miscarriage. It might be because there are four babies percolating inside me and that's what happens sometimes.

But even armed with this new information, I'm not taking more chances than I must. I call my new boss and instead of asking her for the next nine months off, plus maternity leave, plus about 18 years to raise the kids, I go ahead and resign from my new position. Seems like the reasonable thing to do. What do we need with groceries anyway? I'd rather have babies than groceries any old day.

Two days short of being eight weeks pregnant, my thirtieth birthday arrives. None of my clothes fits. I'm already in hand-me-down maternity clothes. My baby bump shows (would it be called a babies bump?), and I look and feel truly pregnant. To get me out of the house and to have a change of scenery, Jason drives me over to my parents for a low-key drop-by visit.

When I walk in and go downstairs, a houseful of people shout, "Surprise!"

My sister Cyndi has planned a surprise party in my parents' backyard. It truly is a complete shock to me. The backyard looks amazing. They've put up a couple of white canopy tents and wrapped ribbons around all the tent poles and the trunks of the many trees in the yard. Candles and lanterns are all over the place, hanging from the tree limbs and scattered among the flower beds and on each of the tables. As the sun sets and the stars come out, the glowing lanterns and candle flames flicker and cast soft yellow light on the faces of friends and loved ones gathered to help me celebrate this milestone birthday. Cyndi serves a fabulous birthday dinner and delicious cake. Eating actually helps my nausea tonight—an unexpected gift in itself—so I can indulge and enjoy the food. The weather is perfect and the ambiance sets my heart to soar. It's a fantastic party and a great way to kick off my new year.

Three weeks after my birthday surprise party, in the eleventh week of my pregnancy, I wake up and the nausea is gone. Just like that. What a relief. I've had enough of lying around. It is time to start nesting.

I begin shopping for baby supplies. At a garage sale, I find a crib and a highchair. A good start. Now I only need three more of each. I take my treasures home to our little 800-square-foot apartment and stockpile them in the second bedroom, which is once again earmarked to become the nursery. I also buy some baby blankets and crib sheets on clearance at Target, but I save the receipts—just in case things don't turn out so well. I am being very practical and unemotional, staying in what I recognize as "nurse mode" and not getting too sentimental about what might be. Though I have confidence that God is with me after he told me so plainly, I realize that it wasn't a promise that all is going to work out to my liking. It's just the assurance that whatever comes, God will be with me through it.

Speaking of whatever comes, Jason is working on getting fired. Actually, not intentionally, but inevitably, nonetheless. He's been working at that minimum-wage job for three months which he loathes. It's a telemarketing company, and he has to make cold calls to angry recipients during their dinner, trying to solicit their patronage. They hate that he calls, but he hates it even more. Overhearing his co-workers make false promises on their calls, exaggerating or making stuff up in order to get the customers to agree, Jason sees how they are making their quotas. They're cheating. But he isn't going to lie or pressure people. So he isn't going to hit his quotas either. He knows his days are numbered there.

On Friday, he calls me and tells me to check the oil and gas up the car; he is on his way home, and we are taking a vacation. He and his supervisor had a little *tête-à-tête*, knowing the end for him there was near, and they both agreed it would be easier if they finished it cleanly, right then and there. A few job possibilities are brewing for him, as he's seen the writing on the wall long enough to get some applications out, but sitting around all weekend isn't going to get anything more accomplished toward getting employed. I call my infertility doctor (who actually is in town this time) to ask permission to travel, and he says if I am going to travel, now is the time. It won't be for another couple of weeks before I start with my new doctor, an obstetrician who is the only doctor in town who has managed and delivered quadruplets, so I don't have his input about travel. But my current doctor seems to believe it's completely fine. Not letting the lack of employment weigh us down, we hit the road and head to Minnesota.

Jason's dad, Jack, and their extended family still live there. In fact, we had moved from Chicago to the family farm for a year before coming to Colorado. So we know plenty of people there and are ready to go spread the exciting news that we are expecting quadruplets. Once we hit Nebraska, we call ahead and let Jack know we're on our way. Oh, the freedom of these early days. So easy to cart four kids around when they are the size of three-inch Kewpie dolls, securely tucked inside of me. We don't need a diaper bag, diapers, bottles, formula, pacifiers, wipes, changing pad, clothes, blankets, car seats, toys, snacks, burp rags, Desitin, cotton balls, q-tips, baby oil, baby soap, baby powder, or any of the other sundries we'll need later when we decide to travel away from home.

It's tremendously enjoyable announcing our news. Everyone is thunderstruck. We go to the home of my good friend Kathy, the obstetrical nurse who trained me and taught me how to deliver a baby when the doctor doesn't arrive in time (which I've had to implement). We laugh marveling over the size of me at only twelve weeks. I already look several months more than that. Her expertise in everything babies makes it especially fun.

Another person we see is Claude, who is about 100 years old (I'm not using hyperbole here—he was actually born in the late nineteenth century). He is the last of his generation around the small farming community. He was Jason's grandpa's best friend, both boys growing up on adjacent farms in the early 1900s. Living next door now to Jack, Claude has no family of his own, has never married, and has no nieces and nephews, so Jack has adopted him as family and watches out for him. Claude's eyesight is lousy, and he can't hear worth beans anymore either, but he won't wear hearing aids because "that's for old people," he says. He talks loudly in low, drawn out vowels—and he rarely speaks to women, pretty typical of the gender segregation you find around these parts. We run into him in the dark, crowded Legion Hall on the one main street that goes through the small town of 729 residents. It's where everyone from the neighboring farms gathers each day to catch up on any news that might have developed since meeting up the previous day.

When Jason practically yells to Claude that we are expecting four babies, Claude lifts his chin to peer at me through his scratched, horn-rimmed glasses, inspecting me for a long beat using the bifocal lenses. In a rare moment, he actually addresses me with his booming voice and Minnesotan accent, saying, "Ah...were you, ah...taking some of those...ah, fertility pills?"

Though I am tired of people asking for the details of how I ended up pregnant with four babies, his question is somehow more tolerable—maybe because of his elderly status—so I kind of smile and holler back at him, "Yes."

He thinks a long moment then looks back at Jason and pronounces, "Well, ah...then...ah...she better stop taking 'em."

We stay around for a long weekend, seeing the good friends we'd made when we lived here, and catching up with the relatives who aren't busy out harvesting their crops. When we return home, good news awaits us. A job is waiting for Jason at Current, Inc., a mail order company. He gets started with orientation, learning the business, and I return to preparing for our expected arrivals.

It's two weeks since our trip to Minnesota and I am exactly fourteen weeks pregnant today, September 17. After my morning shower, I notice something odd is going on with my ever-expanding baby bump. It seems to be contracting a lot, and at rather regular intervals. I've had contractions before, but not like this. As I contemplate this, a distraction comes when the phone rings and on the other end of the line is our good friend from Chicago, David, an academic who lives with his lawyer wife in Georgia now. While we chat, I lounge on my back across our bed, keeping my hand over my children, feeling the muscle tighten beneath my palm. I interrupt our conversation to mention that, oddly enough, I seem to be having regular contractions. Fortunately, brilliant David has his wits about him—unlike me, the former obstetrical and neonatal nurse—and he insists I get off the phone and call my doctor. I can't for the life of me figure out why this didn't occur to me. But I'm thankful David is paying attention. We hang up and I call my obstetrician, the one I've never met. My first appointment with him is scheduled for tomorrow. Turns out, he isn't in the office on Thursdays, so his office nurse tells me to get to the hospital, since I'm timing my contractions now at every fifteen minutes.

Jason is at his first day of work after completing orientation at his new job. And he has the car. So I call Cyndi to ask if she can take me to the hospital, but she isn't home. Fortunately, I'm able to reach my dad since he works evenings and weekends, so he comes and picks me up and takes me in. Not long after we get to the hospital, Jason arrives too. His new boss let him out early.

My nurse at the hospital starts an IV in my arm to hydrate me because extra fluid often helps stop uterine contractions. Then my new doctor comes in to see me, and we meet for the first time. He wants to do a quick ultrasound to make sure the four babies and everything else inside look okay. At the very beginning of the ultrasound, I'm incredibly nervous, nearly panicked. I'm afraid for what he'll find, like maybe not all four hearts still beating. I want him to get started, but I don't want him to. What if they aren't all alive anymore? What will I do? How will I deal with it? I realize my fists are clenched and my shoulder and neck muscles are tense and I'm barely breathing as he goops up my skin and passes the transducer probe over my round belly. My heart speeds up with anxiety. I'm too nervous to ask, but before long I can't wait any longer.

"Are they okay?" I ask, frightened to say it but afraid not to.

He's a quiet, reserved man who doesn't waste words. But at least it doesn't take too long for him to answer that he's satisfied with everyone's condition with a quiet nod. I'll have a more thorough ultrasound later, he tells me, when yet an additional physician will come on board to help manage my care, a perinatologist who specializes in caring for high-risk pregnancies. His office staff will do frequent sonograms to measure the babies and calculate their sizes and make sure they are developing normally.

My new, loquacious obstetrician decides to admit me overnight. "I'm going to keep you overnight," he says quietly without any kind of expression cracking his swarthy Italian face. When I tell him about my appointment tomorrow in his office, he murmurs, "Cancel it." See? Doesn't waste words. While I stay here overnight, they'll keep IV fluids pouring in and make sure things settle down. Dr. Loquacious orders some tests for me as long as I'm going to be around several hours. He wants an EKG and echocardiogram done to establish a baseline in case we have any complications later on. I have a mitral valve prolapse and an arrhythmia they're concerned about, and certain drugs I might need in the future—as well as the fact I'm carrying four babies—can be hard on a person's cardiac status.

The staff explains to me how typically everyone would consider this early "contracting" that I'm experiencing more like cramping, a miscarriage, and they'd let it play out, run its course. But since it's what they're labeling a "valuable pregnancy"—I'm not sure if that's because of how much money it cost us to achieve it or because we really want it—they're going to do what they can to save it. Though they won't call what is happening to me preterm labor since I'm not twenty weeks along yet, they will manage me as though it actually is preterm labor. Currently, I'm the size of a twenty-two week pregnant lady. That's about two months ahead of schedule. Because of the accelerated growth, my uterine muscle has been rapidly stretched and strained, and that's why it's acting up.

Fortunately, the IV hydration all day and all night, plus the "rest" (this hospital bed is one of the worst beds I can remember ever lying in) work as hoped. The contractions subside enough and they discharge me by 2:00 p.m. to go back home, as long as I stay on bed rest, increase my intake of water to about five liters per day, and keep track of my uterine contractions with a home uterine monitor.

A company called Tokos Medical Corporation supplies the equipment needed for home monitoring. It costs thousands of dollars to use, but at least I have good insurance with the COBRA plan I kept after moving from Minnesota where I worked as a labor and delivery nurse. Twice every day, I strap their pricey sensor over my "valuable" baby bump for an hour each time. Once the hour is up, I link the machine to my phone and a nurse in Denver receives the data. She studies the results and lets me know if I am stable or not. If I am contracting too much, she calls back, tells me to drink another liter, and to re-monitor to see if the extra hydration slows down the process.

The rest of the time, I lie around. I'm incubating. That's about all I'm good for right now. And I am going to do it as well as possible. At least the doctor says I can use the bathroom. (By the way, he also tells me he never would have okayed me to go on the trip to Minnesota two weeks ago.) I have to visit the bathroom about every twenty minutes. Try drinking five liters a day, with an occasional extra liter, for kicks. You'll notice trips to the bathroom really pick up. I can also be up long enough to shower once a day, so I do that quickly in the morning before I waddle to the couch and settle in for the remaining hours before bedtime. And that's how you incubate.

CHAPTER 15

THE WEDDING CELEBRATION

The day we got married, Jason and I were apart most of the day running errands and keeping busy with the things one does to get ready for a wedding. With the flowers we'd picked up the day before, Cyndi continued to work furiously in our new kitchen and dining room to arrange our bouquets, boutonnieres, and centerpieces. I left to get my hair done. Jason and some of his family went to pick up his tuxedo and a tank of helium. Instead of our guests lobbing us with rice on our way out of the church, they would release balloons into the Chicago sky. While waiting out the day, many of our out-of-town family were hanging around in our new high-rise apartment that we'd just moved into which was full of moving boxes stacked toward the ceiling. My sister Suzy helped our guests pass the time until the wedding by heading up the crew to unpack our kitchen for us.

For the only time in my life, I'd grown out my fingernails. I went to a salon and got a French manicure. As a violinist who'd started lessons as a young child, I'd only ever had short nails. The new long claws were driving me absolutely crazy, constantly reminding me that I had nail beds by pulling at the quick every time I touched anything. It was like scratching a blackboard every few minutes. But man, they sure looked good. Classy and elegant.

Once I went to the church to get changed, I put on my dress and saw—horror of horrors—panty lines. I had to jettison everything beneath my dress but my lacy white panty hose, otherwise my underclothes showed. Guess that's what I get for doing my own fittings in my little apartment without a full-length mirror. Then I realized soon after redressing that I'd forgotten the rhinestone earrings I'd bought specifically for the special day. There was no time to go home and get them. Cyndi sacrificed her own jewelry for me, handing over her dangling pearly earrings to me without hesitation.

While my bridesmaids and I were waiting for the clock's hour hand to swing around to 5:00 p.m., the church wedding hostess burst into the bridal room in a gusting squall, furious that Jason's sister and her husband were filling balloons with helium in the church basement. I assured the hostess we had no intention of taking any balloons inside the sanctuary, the place she said they'd absolutely not be tolerated. The balloons would go straight from the basement to the front steps outside, where they'd be distributed to our guests right before Jason and I left the church. But she would not countenance having those evil balloons anywhere near that sacred inner sanctum. What if, heaven and God forbid, one got loose inside the church? Determined not to get riled up about it, or let her hysteria ruin my special day, I shrugged, lifting my beautifully manicured hands and my shoulders, and said it was out of my control now. She fumed and spat and stormed back out, vowing something like balloons would be in the church when hell froze over, her exact words fading from my hearing as the door slammed behind her. Even if a balloon did somehow sneak in from outside, past the narthex and through the heavy wooden doors into the sanctuary, then wrest its way out of the hand holding it and float up to the ceiling, by the next morning—merely a Saturday—it would be hovering no more than an inch off the floor. By Sunday it would be a deflated latex blob, a curious shadow beneath a pew, if not already found by the night cleaning crew. It surely wasn't the catastrophic disaster the overbearing woman feared. Knowing Jesus, I don't think he would have minded a balloon inside his house anyway.

The ceremony was lovely, everything unfolding as I'd dreamed. The first half was in candlelight—the lighted candelabras and the flickering flames in the center of our bouquets adding to the golden glow within the breathtaking Gothic Revival sanctuary. The wedding hostess had had her first fit during the rehearsal the previous evening when I told her we were having a candlelight ceremony.

She stated, "No, you're not."

She seemed offended I would even suggest such an outrageous thing. But I dug in my heels and said yes, yes we were. After a back and forth like we were four-year-olds, she huffed but finally compromised by deciding we could have the first part of the wedding in low light. But after that, the lights would have to be turned back up. I don't know why she insisted on the lights being fully illuminated, but I'd already known she had a control problem. A friend who had designed her own veil had argued with this same hostess about which way her headpiece went mere moments before her dad escorted her down the aisle. Yes, *right* as she was about to walk in for the procession. The surly hostess insisted the veil was on backwards and "fixed" it. My friend yanked it back like she'd had it, assuring the hostess that it went *that* way, because she *knew* how it went, because *she had designed the thing herself.*

The pastor who officiated our ceremony was on staff at Fourth Pres. We'd met with him for our required pre-wedding counseling sessions. During one meeting he asked us to name one thing we most admired about each other. Jason offered how dependable I was; if I said I'd do something, he knew it would be done. I was steadfast. The thing he didn't like was that I chewed food with my mouth open. Sometimes. (Apparently.) I couldn't think of anything I didn't like about Jason. I liked his smile. And his acceptance of me as I was; no demands for me to act or be different. Except maybe that chewing thing. The pastor deemed us compatible and gave us the green light to go ahead and get married.

In addition to the primary officiating pastor, my brother-in-law and Jason's brother, both Presbyterian pastors, participated in the ceremony—praying, reading scripture, and leading us as we exchanged vows. My sister Suzy's husband guided me as I recited my vows, and Jason's brother led Jason through his. It was symbolic of our families "giving" each of us away.

The moments that I remember most vividly from the ceremony are the six-minute *Largo* of the Bach Violin Concerto in D minor for Two Violins, or simply the "Bach Double." It was absolutely beautiful. But mostly I remember it because we were kneeling during the music for a time of meditation—and it went on and on. And on. I'd never thought to time the length of the piece. I just knew I loved it. As they played the ethereal, luscious duet, my bent legs began to shake and my ankles and feet went to sleep. I willed myself, *commanded* myself, to pay attention, to ignore my body crying out to stand back up for goodness sake, and to listen and make sure I didn't miss the music I'd so highly anticipated. I was determined not to let my mind wander. It was only by sheer force of will that I was able to keep my attention on the music and off my legs. And the struggle paid off. See? I remember it.

After we were pronounced married, the fabulous *rondeau* brass fanfare (Masterpiece Theatre's signature tune) resounded and we recessed with wide smiles up the white aisle runner. We'd taken photos before the ceremony so there wouldn't be a long wait between the wedding and the reception. The two of us snuck into the courtyard by the fountain to have a little alone time while our guests exited, and Jason's sister handed out the balloons to everyone congregating on the front steps. I found out later that my seventy-eight-year-old grandmother got cold waiting and stepped inside the narthex for a moment to warm up. The wedding hostess was lurking inside and kicked Grandma back out with a thorough scolding for coming in with her balloon. My poor cold grandma. A shivering little old lady, clutching a white balloon and looking for a moment's relief from the autumn chill. Some hostess.

With the signal it was time, we burst through the heavy oaken doors to emerge for the first time as Mr. and Mrs. We descended the concrete steps to cheers and applause, and everyone released their green and white balloons that floated away with their beribboned tales waving high over our heads past the stone spire. They drifted on the crisp breeze blowing in off the lake—blobs of green and white noiselessly shrinking from sight above the sounds of Chicago rush-hour traffic. In black tuxedo and trailing wedding gown train, Jason and I walked hand in hand down the sidewalk as a Michigan Avenue bus roared up and clanked open its squeaky bi-fold doors. Our wedding guests thought we were going to board CTA's 151, but when we reached it, we turned the opposite way (unaware that it looked like we were heading right for it). Instead of getting on the bus, we aimed for the idling limousines parked around the corner of the church, waiting to take us and the wedding party to the Holiday Inn.

The reception was a tremendous celebration with 200 friends and relatives from all over the country. Too wound up to eat, I only picked at a few bites of the food, though I did work a little harder to eat the chocolate mousse. Of course. The three-tiered cake was beautiful, but it wasn't the chocolate flavor I was looking forward to. I *love* chocolate cake. But ours was dry and more like a spice cake that they'd forgotten to add the cloves and cinnamon to. The bakery apologized later and refunded half of what they'd charged me. We kept the top layer anyway and froze it for our first anniversary. (It tasted a year's worth of freezer burn worse, but it was fun.) The string quartet was fabulous and made the reception dinner elegant and refined. And my baby sister—nine years old—played her first violin concerto as a bonus treat for our dinner guests, accompanied by my dad on his violin. Our friend David was mightily impressed with my sister. He had good reason to be impressed—since her music sounded so much like Bach. Which it was, actually. David thought her "first concerto"—as my dad had introduced it to the crowd—meant it was her first violin concerto *composition*. But she hadn't written it. She was simply performing for her first time one of Bach's concertos.

After a wonderful evening of beautiful music, delicious food (so they told me), laughter, and merriment, Jason and I said goodbye to everyone and went to the elevator to go up to our nearly-a-$700-value suite. Upstairs, we found that our room had been thoroughly sprinkled with rice—between the sheets, in the sinks and tub, over the furniture, and in our personal belongings. In the process of discovering where all the rice was, we found that there were none of my things there to be covered with rice. One particular person in my family who will remain nameless had been charged with making sure someone delivered our luggage to our room before the reception. But my bag apparently didn't make the trip. Instead we had other people's stuff—my nine-year-old sister's clothes and some odds and ends in a brown paper grocery sack my bridesmaids had left after we changed at the church. To get home the next day, I cobbled together an outfit of a denim miniskirt and someone's (I think my little sister's) pink fuzzy sweater. I had to wear the only shoes I had, which were my high-heeled white pumps. The closest thing I had to underwear was my lacy white pantyhose, since I'd had to jettison everything else before the wedding because of the panty lines. In my fuzzy sweater, denim miniskirt, white lace hose and pumps, I looked exactly like a hooker. A hooker with no fashion sense whatsoever. When we hailed a cab to go back to our apartment where our out-of-town family was waiting for us, Jason got in the taxi with what looked a lot more like a tasteless companion than his new bride.

That night—Saturday—Jason's three boat buddies and their wives (the guys had all gained spouses the previous year) threw a *bon voyage* dinner party for us on the penthouse floor of one of their buildings. It gave us another chance after the reception to spend time and celebrate with close friends and family who'd traveled so far for the wedding.

On Sunday everyone returned to their home states— just in time for me to get a stomach bug. I lay around on the couch unable to eat anything and hoping I wouldn't throw up again. On Monday we were scheduled to leave for London for our honeymoon. We nearly cancelled but in the end, we decided to make a go of it since the worst seemed to be behind me, and I'd just be sleeping another twelve hours on the plane anyway. I hardly ate for the first few days in England, but everyone knows you don't go to England for its food. Tea and toast got me through just fine.

We stayed in England for ten unforgettable days. As we walked around London one afternoon, a man stopped us and told us to pose for his camera. He took some pictures, then said he'd send them to us. He handed us a notebook, telling us to write down our address. When we gave it back, he said in his lovely British accent, "That will be four pounds then." Jason and I looked at each other skeptically. We knew it was probably a con, but we weren't in a mood to quibble. Why not? It was only four pounds. Maybe he needed it more than we did.

During our trip we toured the Tower of London in the rain (that really shortened long lines), shopped at Harrods and Laura Ashley, visited Canterbury, walked among

Roman ruins, attended performances of both *Chess* and *Mousetrap* in the West End, and saw the real England, guided by my elderly British cousin Joe who lived outside of London with his wife Florrie. They hosted us for a few of the days we were in the country. Florrie eagerly greeted us while we were still in bed each morning, serving us a tea tray and throwing wide the curtains to let the sunshine in, giving us quite an authentic English experience. She enjoyed sherry every night, saying in her Cockney accent after each drink, "I feel it in me eyes."

About a month after we got home, an international package came in the mail. Inside were four different photographs of Jason and me posing on a London street. What a guy. The photographer wasn't a con after all.

CHAPTER 16

NOTES ON BEING
A TURNIP

It's been only four days since my little not-called-preterm-labor-yet incident that landed me in the hospital. While I'm doing my incubating on the couch, trying my best to remain sedentary and peaceful, the doorbell rings. On the other side of the screen is one of those people in uniform shorts who delivers registered letters. *How exciting.* I love surprises. I sign for it and waddle back to the couch and tear into my letter.

Oh, dear. It's from my insurance company.

Like a good patient, I'd called them during my first trimester to let them know I'm pregnant with quadruplets. The lady on the other end of the phone was so lovely and glad to talk to me. She was quite interested in my story and asked lots of questions. It was fun to share. We chatted and laughed and had a delightful conversation. She explained that soon I would receive a call from a special agent who would manage my case. I felt so cared for, so watched out for.

With this letter it seems my specially assigned agent is trying to manage me right out of my coverage. Since my call to them, my insurance company has apparently been scrambling to find a way out of being my insurance company. According to my special telegram, my special agent has dug around until finding a way to drop me from my plan coverage.

This is what my special letter says.

Dear Mrs. Gillard:

It has been brought to my attention that you had other insurance coverage through ——— Corporation while you were enrolled under our coverage.

This is code for, "We figured out that you're about to have some hefty medical bills and we don't want anything to do with you if we can possibly get away with it."

The terrible, horrible, no good, very bad letter goes on:

Our guidelines state that once you're eligible for other insurance coverage, you are no longer eligible to continue under our coverage. Since you were covered through the ——— Corporation effective January 1, you became ineligible for our coverage on that date.

This means, "Oh, yay. We think we found a big, round loophole through which we can heave you." They are talking about my job as a maternal-child homecare nurse, saying that I had insurance as their employee. In point of fact, I wasn't covered by that job's offered insurance, as they're claiming. It was optional. And I chose to stay with the insurance I had under COBRA, the better insurance.

Which apparently isn't better, if you rate them by how they are acting now.

It probably goes without saying, but I will say it anyway. *I am freaking out.*

At the end of the letter, the nice lady writing tells me to feel free to call her with any questions. So special. Oh yeah, and she said to have a nice day, or some stupid crazy advice like that. *Ha! Nice day, my foot.*

I do call them. As soon as I can catch my breath. Not only does the nice lady confirm (with a smile I can absolutely hear in her voice) that they are canceling my coverage, but they are doing it retroactively and they intend to demand repayment of all claims paid from January 1 to date. That was almost *ten months* ago.

Do you recall that little episode with the fluid problem in my belly and lungs back in February and March? That was a $25,000 episode, for which this particular company had covered most of the hospital claims. They want it all back. Not to mention the overnight stay I just had at the hospital, along with all those expensive tests, and the pricey daily home monitoring they prescribed that I've been using at home.

Gulp.

I am unemployable. And Jason only has his new minimum-wage job, which doesn't even offer medical benefits for his current position. (Remember how he had been a commercial commodities broker in Chicago at PaineWebber, that large brokerage firm that wasn't Merrill Lynch? His new job is *nothing* like that was.) And my infertility doctor has all our money, plus dibs on the first kid, if it's cute enough. We certainly don't have tens of thousands of dollars hanging around to give back to the insurance company, nor the money to cover the future expenses without insurance. As it is, we are paying $200 a month to keep me eligible and in good standing with this corporation that's trying to stiff us. That $200 premium, plus rent, more than uses up our paltry monthly income.

Until Jason gets home from work, I try not to outright panic. I struggle not to start screaming at the ceiling. Or go crazy. Or into labor. When Jason finally arrives, I shove the letter in his face.

He reads it and quietly contemplates for a time. He decides first to call his dad. Jack used to be a lawyer and a judge, so he knows a thing or two. Jason also calls Mike, his best man at our wedding, who is a lawyer in corporate law.

Their consensus: you can't squeeze blood from a turnip.

This is supposed to comfort me?

First of all, I have never heard this phrase. But once I ponder it, I figure it out. I am the turnip, and some huge corporation is about to squish me to a bloodless pulp. This is not a very good thing to say to a pregnant woman with more hormones raging through her system then any given man will produce in a lifetime.

So Mike, Jack, the wife of David-who-made-me-call-my-doctor who is a lawyer in Georgia, and my older sister Suzy who works for a law firm in Texas, are helping me research so we can draft a letter to address the whole issue. After a few hours, we talk to Mike again, and he actually manages to calm me quite a bit, assuring me once again that turnips don't bleed. A peace has come over me that has replaced that initial terrible, horrible dread of doom.

After searching many documents and reading multiple forms and digging into the fine print of the fine print, we discover that I wasn't actually required to accept new insurance if its coverage didn't provide for pre-existing conditions. And that is the case. The new insurance wouldn't have covered me for my pre-existing endometriosis. So I wasn't required, after all, to have given up my COBRA coverage when the other insurance became available.

I write back to the nice lady—with the help of my excellent, wonderful, so good, very best law team—and carefully point out where their strategy is flawed. All they needed to do was read the very tiny, tiny print in their own contracts. Then I go on to tell them in my letter that their actions are making my already challenging pregnancy much more difficult, and that they are contributing to my anxiety level, which is obviously harmful to my physical and mental health, and subsequently to the health of my four unborn babies. I tell them I expect the situation to be resolved satisfactorily, or I will hold them responsible for any detrimental health effects attributable to their actions. Then I throw around a few names of partners in law firms (the senior partner from my sister's law firm has come on board to help us) and finish up by cc'ing everyone I can think of after my signature on the letter, including the commissioners of insurance for both Colorado and Minnesota.

I have no idea what they will do with all of this. It feels more than a little audacious to include the insurance commissioners, but I also feel empowered in a way. I can only hope. In the meantime, still the penniless pregnant turnip that I am, I need to look for other possible ways to pay for these babies. It will be a shame to get through the whole thing and then have to sell them all to pay for the cost of having them. Plus, the infertility doctor still has claim to the one, if he wants it.

So I make a call to Social Services, certainly not something I want to do, or have even thought of doing before this whole insurance debacle. But we have little choice now.

Hallelujah. It turns out that there is indeed a new program for which we can apply to receive medical coverage. Eligibility will be based on our meager income, and it would cover me during the pregnancy and the kids for the year following their birth. Plus, the bonus is, if we *have* insurance, this program will pay the premiums to keep us covered and then act as a secondary insurance, which will cost the program much less in the long run. So whether things get cleared up with my COBRA or not, we might have found some help.

CHAPTER 17

THE CHICAGO LIFE

We loved living in Chicago. What a great town. And the friends we had—so many who would become lifelong friends with whom we are in contact still. For our first two years of married life, we lived in a high-rise in a fantastic neighborhood in Lincoln Park, right next to Lincoln Park Zoo (which has free admission, by the way). We lived in a corner two-bedroom on the ninth floor with floor-to-ceiling windows on two full sides of the apartment—freezing cold in the frigid windy Chicago winters but man, the view was tremendous.

The apartment was only a half mile from my hospital. I was working nights, half of my shifts twelve hours long. After every six weeks, I switched to two weeks on the day shift. A year after we were married, my schedule changed to four weeks on nights, then four weeks on days. Plus, I still worked every other weekend. Jason worked his white-collar job down in the Loop, a regular sort of nine-to-five schedule. The third year, I transferred from the NICU to pediatric surgery, with ten-hour shifts in the OR, four days a week and *no weekends*. When I had my weekday off and Jason was at work, I often stayed in bed reading for much of the day, waiting for him to get home so we could go play.

We loved to eat out. Our favorite restaurants included: the Imperial Cathay for Chinese food, where we *mmm*'d over the moo shu pork in paper-thin pancakes smeared with extra duck sauce; Boston Blackie's, the low-lit bistro with small tables coated in inch-thick polyurethane and burgers so big they were the size of the plates; Santa Fe Barbecue, whose racks of ribs were soaked in sauce that, as we ate, dripped over the beans and slaw, and the rolls were softer than cotton candy and slathered with honey-butter. For pizza, we alternated between Giordano's and Bacino's, each with crust thick enough our jaws popped getting our teeth around it. Let's Dog It and its imported secret red relish and chili served over Vienna all-beef franks from its street side café was a favorite. And of course, Mrs. Field's Cookies, the confectionary staple that helped us fall in love. Soft chewy chocolate chip cookies that demanded you close your eyes and stop talking to eat properly. Before we'd officially started dating, and before I knew that Jason loved chocolate as much as I did, I bought a bag of Mrs. Field's cookies and took them to one of our church meetings. Clandestinely, I gave Jason a sneak peek of the sack, wiggled my eyebrows, and asked him in a whisper if he wanted some. With a grin, he nodded enthusiastically. We made our excuses and left to enjoy some dessert by ourselves, where we could devour the entire contents without sharing with anyone else.

Some evenings while I was at the hospital taking care of sick neonates, Jason was at classy restaurants or sporting events wining and dining clients, like Japanese investment bankers. Other times, when the firm had tickets but no clients to entertain, they gave away the tickets to Jason, and the two of us got to enjoy them. We went to see the Blackhawks and Bulls, sitting so close to Michael Jordon that we had to dodge sweat splattering over those of us sitting on the court floor in seats just behind the sidelines.

We loved going to baseball games. My favorite was the Cubs, and we often went to Wrigley Field to watch Andre Dawson, Ryne Sandberg, and Shawon Dunston while Harry Caray commentated and led us in the Seventh Inning Stretch sing-along. Jason was a life-long Minnesota Twins fan, so we sometimes went to the South Side to Comiskey Park to see Kirby Puckett and his Twins teammates when they were in town to beat the White Sox.

Interested in trying new things, we went with our friends, David and Betsey, to the horse races at Arlington Park in the northwest suburb of Arlington Heights. For fun, we made two-dollar bets on horses we picked mostly by closing our eyes and pointing at the list of competing contenders. Once or twice we won a few dollars, making it a wash. Another race we enjoyed was an annual event put on by one of my coworkers and friends, Paul. Every year at a bay along Lake Geneva, Wisconsin, he and his wife hosted homemade milk carton boat races and an elaborate cookout for his extended family and a few of us lucky friends. During the races, Paul waded into the cold, waist-deep water with his clipboard to follow the fleet of competing crafts to monitor the tournament and determine the winners in each of his categories. Our boats never won any speed records, and one wouldn't even stay upright (too buoyant, needing more keel weight we discovered once launched), but we did get a prize for decorative design for our boat the "Columbia," which had an eighteen-inch wide Viking-style sail and a proud woman figurehead at the bow holding up her fist in defiance. At the end of the day after the sun set, Paul lit a roaring bonfire, and we toasted marshmallows over the burning boats.

We also enjoyed walking. We walked all over Chicagoland, miles and miles on many days. We explored west side neighborhoods, searching for architecturally interesting buildings like old movie theaters and renovated (or not) storefronts. The lakeshore beach and Lakeshore Drive were fun to traverse. Sometimes we hoofed it from Lincoln Park to Water Tower Place, not to shop but to check out the stores in the eight-story mall, or we went to another multi-storied mall on Clark Street, one with a lot of exposed ductwork and other interesting structural elements in the open helix design. Ace Hardware was another favorite to roam around. They had the coolest merchandise, from housewares and appliances to electronics and knickknacks.

Once when I was working the weekend day shift with two twelves back-to-back (I'd work, go home and sleep, and go back to work to start over), I crawled out of the warm bed on a cold Sunday morning in October—abandoning Jason to comfortably snooze away without me—and threw on some sweats. (I'd change into scrubs at the hospital.) Cold and silent, I walked the four deserted blocks along the dusky streets of Chicago between our apartment and Children's. I walked into the lobby, looked over at the security guard's desk, and spied the clock over his head. And moaned. I'd come in at 6:00 a.m., totally forgetting we'd gained an hour for Daylight Saving Time. Since we lived so close, I spun around and marched right back to our apartment. I climbed into the cozy bed next to

Jason's warmth and went to sleep for all of fifteen minutes. Then I had to pry myself out of the snug bed all over again. I should have stayed in the hospital lobby and read a magazine, or simply stared at a wall for an hour.

When our property manager raised the rent for our high-rise more than we wanted to shell out, we moved into a quaint framed walkup five blocks west and two blocks north. The house had been converted into two apartments, ours on the top floor, with the basement as a common area shared with the tenants on the first floor—people we hardly heard except for their occasional thumping music and the resonant voice of their giant talking parrot. It lived on an enormous perch in their living room, visible through the sheers of their front window.

Our flat was long and narrow, close enough to our next door neighbors that we could carry on a conversation with them through our adjacent windows (or hear them making love, depending on the hour). Our apartment had parquet floors, tall ceilings, a fireplace, and a lot of sunshine.

It was a marvelous place to live—except for the rodents. One evening sitting at our dining table having dinner, a bold mouse scampered out into the open and zipped across the room, coming precariously close to my foot. We named the mouse Jerry, based on my favorite cartoon as a kid. (Sorry, Mickey.) A little piece of advice: never name something you'll end up needing to kill. (See Mickey? Not so bad after all.) To ease the nasty task of exterminating Jerry, we put out those sticky traps, instead of the snap-break-its-neck type. (We didn't know that the quick way was actually the more humane, less traumatic way—for everyone involved.) It turned out that Jerry had invited a bunch of his friends inside to warm their little paws too. We called them all Jerry. Each day, once we both got home from work, we'd have a Jerry Report to check in and update each other about any Jerry sighting or catches.

One fateful day, one of the Jerries got his leg stuck in the glue of a sticky trap, then he dragged it under the fridge, and the trap got hung up, too big to fit beneath the edge. Freaked me out, I tell you, seeing that trap jerk around down at the bottom of the appliance with a mouse on the other end pulling on it. It made me not want to be in the same house as any Jerry. We decided we better get him out from under there somehow, to do what with, I didn't know. Catch and release? Whack him on the head with a spatula? What a dumb idea glue traps are.

Fortunately, Jerry got himself off the trap before we could intervene. I was relieved. I didn't want to even *look* at him, let alone watch his fight to get away or whack him on the little head. *Be free. Run like the wind.* What harm, really, was he doing anyway?

Soon after Jerry escaped, the neighbors below us moved out. Curious (and nosy), we went downstairs to check out their emptied apartment. As we walked the hallway toward their living room, the sound of our footsteps echoed between the bare wood floors and the stripped walls.

Whoa, those former neighbors were clearly not going to get their deposit back from Carl, our landlord. Their parrot had been a messy eater. Bird seed was *everywhere* in that vacant room, strewn across the parquet as though the tenants had walloped open a piñata full of sunflower seeds, showering the room with husks and hulls. No wonder we'd had an infestation of Jerries.

Once Carl swept up the mess, then scrubbed and polished the wood back to an immaculate shine, he had the place ready and a new tenant moved in. And we never had any more Jerries come to dinner.

CHAPTER 18

NOTES ON BEING RELIEVED

A week passes while I wait and wonder if I am going to get my insurance coverage back, and if I'm going to be accepted into the Medicaid program. My anxiety dashes in and out of my awareness as I try to cope and keep my mind off the worries and stresses by doing cross-stitch, reading, or watching Star Trek reruns.

Today is our fifth wedding anniversary. It's certainly not a typical day of celebration for us. Not with me a bloated whale marooned on the couch. Though we can't go out, one thing we can do that we've done each year on our anniversary is to page through our wedding photo album, look at the pictures from London including the snapshots from the street photographer who wasn't a con, and read a cherished little book we filled out when we got married about how we met, our first date and impressions, our favorite things about each other, favorite foods, best places to go, and other memories. It's fun and a good distraction, though a cloud of worry still lingers over my head. In spite of trying to remain calm and unperturbed about my perilous insurance status, I am having too many contractions to ignore, and I feel pretty crummy. It feels like my chest is getting squished and like something is not normal. Well, my chest *is* getting squished. And it's *not* normal to have multiple people growing inside of me trying to make more room for themselves by invading farther up into my rib cage. So I guess the discomfort is to be expected. But still, it doesn't feel good.

When I make a call to my OB because of feeling so lousy, his office nurse tells me to come in for an unscheduled check-up to make sure everything is okay. I go in, and his office manager informs me that my doctor doesn't see Medicaid patients. But this time, for me he'll make an exception. Amazing how quickly insurance status can change one from being a desired, regarded patient into someone who is marginalized and rejected. Suddenly, neither I nor my pregnancy is feeling all that valued. I'm not sure if they will keep me only until everything is worked out with my insurance, or if they will continue to treat me even if it turns out I have no private insurance. Everything is in upheaval. I'm trying hard to keep my panic in check. *Breathe deeply. Evenly.* One of the last things I need is for my doctor to dump me too.

The nurse escorts Jason and me into a small room. I change into paper clothes and sit to wait on the end of the table covered by crinkly butcher paper, resting my palm on my baby bump to feel if it's still contracting. When the doctor comes in, he greets us with his usual subdued, serious face. He examines me and checks the babies, making sure everything is okay. Since my last visit with him only nine days ago—back when I was a qualified, acceptable patient—I've gained four pounds, and the height of my fundus (the top of a uterus used to measure the stage of a pregnancy) has grown another three centimeters. (About one centimeter per week is normal.) I'm as big as someone ten weeks further along than I really am. It's as though I'm attached to a tire pump that is inflating me like a giant beach ball. The rapid expansion certainly explains my physical misery.

As the visit unfolds, I'm relieved to sense that my doctor isn't treating me any differently or interacting with me like things have changed. Because he's such a taciturn, reserved fellow, any shift might not be perceivable. Even this early in our association, I've recognized that he's not a typical sort of physician. And I've known a lot of them after plenty of years working in hospitals and having so many different doctors care for me. Like for one thing, he never wears socks. Even when he's wearing a suit. He always wears leather loafers. Probably expensive Italian leather. He's Italian, so why not? All the doctors I've known wear socks. He's unconventional. So maybe it doesn't even make any real difference to him if I'm poor or kicked off my insurance. Maybe his no-Medicaid-patients policy is something his office manager pushes to make sure the staff gets paid and the lights stay on. Maybe my atypical doctor ignores those details—which would be nice, since I really want him as my doctor, because he's the only one around with quadruplet experience.

He proclaims me and my babies well enough and sends me home again to lie back down.

The next day, the doorbell rings and FedEx is back with a second envelope delivery telling me that my letter to my unscrupulous insurance company has been forwarded to a senior vice president. (They don't call themselves unscrupulous. I'm adding that in myself.) The VP will be thoroughly researching the matter and get back to me.

Great. More waiting.

But it only takes a day. I receive the third registered letter which says:

We are pleased to inform you that your coverage will continue...

Ha! My crack legal team did it. What a relief.

Two days later, the call comes in from Medicaid. They've accepted us! So now I have secondary insurance that will begin picking up the $200 a month we have been paying out to keep my primary insurance, plus cover the leftover bills after the first insurance pays its portion. This is *huge*. We will have enough money after paying rent to buy bread and eggs. And we won't have to sell any of the kids. We are feeling grand.

What a cool thing. I believe it is God who has turned a potentially nasty problem into a much better situation. One of those redemption of bad things at least, if not outright direct provision for our needs, plain and simple. None of this relief would have come about if it hadn't been for that nice lady trying to shove me out the loophole.

MERRY CHRISTMAS FROM THE GILLARDS 1990

CHAPTER 19

THE MOVE TO HOMELESSNESS

By the time we'd been a year in our cozy walkup, Jason had lived in Chicago for more than seven years, and I'd been there over five. We loved Chicago, yet we were beginning to feel the restlessness that can come with routine and predictability. Thinking of starting a family made us contemplate where we'd want to raise children and consider moving out of the big city. Jason was interested in trading commodities on his own, and I had graduated from nursing school with the dream of working in obstetrics, something I had yet to achieve.

Jason's dad, Jack, was in the process of knocking down the century-old drafty farmhouse on the family farm in Minnesota to replace it with a new house big enough for the extended family to live in—Jack said he wanted us to be like the Ewings on the TV show *Dallas* where everyone lived together—and he invited us to come and make a life there in rural America. (He wanted the togetherness, not the feuding.)

The peaceful serenity of the countryside struck a chord with us. And sharing the cost of living with Jason's dad and stepmom would allow Jason to set up his own business to trade commodities. We decided to do it.

To prepare, we visited the farm to talk details with Jack and also help empty the old farmhouse to prepare for demolition. In the mosquito-infested swampy summer heat, we transferred everything up into the hot airless loft of the barn and Jason's dad and stepmom moved into a small office building next to the barn. A few weeks later, the bulldozer came. The monumental moment of the bulldozer crashing down the historic house, which originally was a hotel, is forever preserved in our jerky Super 8 home movies. The much-anticipated razing meant we were actually going to do this. Two months before our planned move, we returned again to check on the progress of the new house, something Jack told us was coming along just fine.

When we saw that "progress," we were taken aback. Or maybe dismayed would be more accurate. A shallow hole of dark tilled soil outlined the footprint of the new house-to-be. It was the only thing there. But Jack assured us it was all fine; we should move forward with our plans to relocate. The builders were due any day. Less than ten days later they poured the concrete, and the foundation and basement walls were standing. Jack sent us a Polaroid to show the progress. It was moving swiftly now. There would be a place for us, Jack said. So Jason and I each took a deep breath and handed in our notices at work. Jack gave us updates along the way, affirming that all was fine, and he was looking forward to our arrival.

To get us and our belongings there, we rented a one-way Ryder truck and arranged with a moving company to hire three of their burly men to come load it for us. Living on the second floor, we didn't have any inclination to move everything down the steps ourselves, especially if we could have burly helpers.

The morning of the move arrived, and we picked up the truck, double parked it out in front of the house, and worked on packing the final odds and ends inside while we waited for those burly movers to come.

And we waited.

And waited.

When I called the moving company, they told me there was a mix-up, but two guys would be there soon.

When I called again later, they said there'd been another delay; it wouldn't be long now.

When I called a third time, they told me oh, yeah, they'll be there. But my BS radar went off. I said, "Level with me here. I have a truck out there and it needs loading. If you don't have guys to send me, tell me right now because the day is wasting, and I need that truck loaded."

They said, "Well no, there is no one coming." Great. Just great.

Jason and I would have to pretend to be burly movers ourselves. Time to get to work. We had an apartment to empty and a truck to load.

The heavy items needed to go onto the truck first, so we wrestled the washer and dryer out of the basement and up the back steps using a dolly. Then we had the sleeper sofa. Oh, the sleeper sofa. Anyone who has ever moved a sleeper sofa has no doubt cursed the day the inventor of the sleeper sofa was ever born. The hefty couch was more weight than we wanted to carry all the way out the back and around the entire house—even though the back had a

169

wider stairwell—so we decided we'd go straight out the front door, avoiding the distance and all those turns. It started out okay. But have you ever moved one of those monsters?

As we hauled the sofa down our staircase to the door inside the front entrance, it got heavier and heavier, and lower and lower. And I think the stairwell walls got closer and closer. We couldn't hold it up at the right angle to put that unwieldy peg through that narrow hole at the end of the stairway. By the time we reached the bottom, the thing was wedged in so tightly, we couldn't back up, couldn't lift it, nor could we go forward. With the angle it was at, it was just plain stuck.

It was about that time our friend Mary came by to see how progress was. We were easy to find. The big empty yellow truck in the middle of the street and us, stuck at the front door with a sleeper sofa wedged in the doorway.

Mary knew some guys from her violin making school who she thought might want to earn some extra cash, so she said she'd go make some phone calls and try to drum up a couple of movers for us. Meanwhile, we used our problem-solving skills and spatial relations acumen to figure out what to do. We only needed about an inch to clear that narrow opening, so we decided to take apart the doorway. By removing the trim and then the door jamb, we could open the doorway by enough room to push that monster through. We finally got the couch out when Carl, our landlord, called and asked if he could drop off our deposit check. Oh, my gosh. You know the "deposit check," the one he only gives back if everything—like the front doorway—is in good shape, intact, like when we moved in? We had to scramble. He only lived next door. With newfound energy, we threw the doorway back together, returned the trim, and started nailing it back in place. When Carl arrived, we weren't quite done. We stood right in front of the door as he shook our hands (the hands not behind our backs holding hammers), said goodbye, and wished us luck. I barely heard what he said because I was busy hoping like crazy that the trim wouldn't fall off and hit Carl in the face.

After an hour or two, three of the skinniest guys you've ever seen (they were *violin makers*, for goodness' sake) arrived to empty our apartment into the truck. But I guess it didn't matter that they weren't big burly movers. By then, we'd already heaved all the heavy stuff into the truck.

When finally our apartment was emptied and we'd finished cleaning, it was late in the day. Exhausted but ready to start our adventure, we said goodbye to Mary and bid farewell to Chicago. We drove as far as Wisconsin and stayed overnight in a motel. On that next day in the autumn of 1990, we finally arrived at the farm, ready to take a breath of the fresh country air, unload our things, and enjoy our new lodgings.

But the only thing there to greet us was a shell of a house: dirt floor, open studs, and outer plywood walls with only roughed-in empty window openings. No electricity, no plumbing, no *rooms*. No one was at the farm, so Jason and I walked around the yard shaking our heads, trying to wrap our minds around what we had just done.

We were still in shock and unsure how to address the devastation when Jack finally got home late that day. I whined to him, "But you said there was a place for us."

"But there is," he said with a smile. "Pastor Bates said you can stay in his guest bedroom. It's all arranged. He knows you're coming tonight."

"But what about *tomorrow* night?" I cried.

"He said you can stay for as long as you need," Jack assured me. "He's fine with that."

CHAPTER 20

NOTES ON BEING CREATIVE

I can't believe it's already halfway through October. Now at eighteen weeks, it's time to meet our new perinatologist. He and his team, along with my obstetrician, will help me stay pregnant and healthy as long as humanly possible. He has a much different personality from Dr. Loquacious, and he tells us right off to call him by his first name, Bob. I like him. (I like them *both*, I want to be clear.) Bob smiles a lot, is warm, and makes us feel very much at home and well-cared for. He is optimistic about me staying home a while yet. Maybe I can even stay until after Thanksgiving. (Also, he wears socks, in case you're wondering.)

At the appointment with Bob and his staff of high-risk pregnancy pros, we have a different, more advanced kind of specialized ultrasound to evaluate each baby. They visualize and check the babies physically—hearts and kidneys, spines, and bladders—all things they use to track development and status (the good news right up front is they look like they're supposed to). Then they measure the length of their femurs and the size of their heads. They plug the numbers into formulas to estimate their weight, length, and overall health. Each baby is in the ballpark of nearly half a pound and close to eight inches long. While the pros do their high-tech assessments and calculations, we get to see our kids' little bodies—fingers and toes, ribs and limbs, faces and movement, plus the position of each one of them inside of me. They wiggle and squirm throughout the entire two-and-a-half-hour exam, kicking their legs, batting their arms, and clearly playing a game of soccer.

We also find out their genders. I'm lying on the table with Jason by my side watching the white and gray shadows of our babies' tiny forms. The first baby is identified by the ultrasound tech as a boy. The next one, the biggest of the four, is a girl. Perfect. One boy, one girl. Just like it's supposed to be. The next one, a boy again. Then the fourth? A boy? Wait. When I hear the verdict, disappointment sinks my enthusiasm. How can it be? That's not good. Two days ago, my new friend who has one-year-old quadruplets came over to visit me, show me pictures of her kids, and to get better acquainted. When I asked her what she had, *boys? girls? both?*, she answered, "Two of each. It's perfect." So as I'm lying on the table I can only think of her words, that two of each is perfect, meaning anything different *isn't* perfect, right? I'm trying not to be distressed. Her words are impacting me way too much. It's crazy. Who says it has to be that way? Why can't three and one be okay, even good? I muster my adult brain, banish from my thoughts the misconstrued concept, and embrace our new information. This is going to be fine. This is going to be good.

Knowing now which baby is a girl and who are the boys, we decide to name them. There is so much you can do when you get to name four kids at once. Jason's family has a tradition of giving babies two middle names, but we opt out of that because coming up with *twelve* good names is simply going to be too much to pull off. For years on our cross-country road trips, we've played a game collecting unusual place or business names from road signs to use for any future kids. But now that we're actually here and need to decide what to call our children, that odd collection seems a little too weird. We don't really want a girl named Shar-Lee or sons named Horace and Clyburn. (No offense intended, Shar-Lee or Clyburn.)

During the naming process, we consider alliteration. I was friends with identical triplets in elementary school, three carbon-copy girls who all had "K" names—Konny, Karmen, and Kerry. It made an already challenging identification process more difficult. And another factor, I remember well how when I was a kid, when my mom was exasperated with me or one of my siblings and was yelling at us, she'd trip over all of our names—and often the dog's or cat's thrown in to boot—getting only more frustrated not being able to quickly call out whoever was busted. And only *some* of ours began with the same sounds. Starting everyone's name the same only makes yelling at your kids a lot harder. *Frank— Fred— Fido— Fanni— for heaven's sake. Fergus. Take that bean out of your nose!* That won't do us any favors. Jason and I readily agree to rule out alliteration.

We play around with biblical names, because, why not? The best we can come up with is Matthew, Mark, Luke, Ann-John. Though good for a few laughs, the holy set of monikers is sure to bring only regret in time. It'd be like dressing them in matching clothes all the way into high school. I won't be that nerdy of a mom and doom my kids to being bullied. No, I want to be a mom cool enough that my kids won't make me drop them off for school three blocks away from the building.

There is always rhyming. I love rhymes, but in Dr. Seuss books, where they should probably stay. Jason and I joke about Larry, Harry, Jerry, and Mary. And we even tell some people those are the names we've chosen so they won't ask anymore. It works. They give us funny tight smiles, nod, and say no more. We don't want any feedback from anyone that will influence us or make us question our choices while we're still trying to figure out what we really think ourselves.

After plenty of goofing around, we get serious and start brainstorming to come up with eight agreeable and durable names. We make lists of family names. We write down grandparents, great-grandparents, matriarchal maiden names, and names we just like. Jason likes the tradition of using a mother's maiden name as a first name. But I don't want a son named Robinson. I worked with one once. Once you know someone, the name becomes them. I can't reconcile my kid with a huge middle-aged hairy guy named Robinson.

I like the idea of using Jason's middle name for a boy. And I feel a tad bit obligated to use it because I basically forbade my sister-in-law from taking it when she had a son a year ago and considered it for him. I declared it was ours to use, since it was Jason's name. As she is always wont to be, she was gracious about it and laughed and chose something else. Now I better make good use of it.

Among ancestors on both sides of our family, we find several inspirations. We decide early on to avoid Irving, Ida, and Frank, some of Jason's grandparents' names. We want our kids to like us, after all. (We know. One day they'll be thirteen. But I mean for the other years.) For our daughter, we settle on derivations of my grandma and great-grandma, Mary and Bessie, choosing Molly Elizabeth. For the boys, we come up with five family names we like well enough to use. Three are from grandfathers and great-grandfathers: Spencer, Thomas, and Charles. Plus Jason's middle name, Pierce (the one I called dibs on). And one is my other grandmother's maiden name, Whitney. We still have room for one wild card. We've used up the family names we like. We could reconsider Horace, but again, we do want them to like us later on.

We start pairing up names to see which go together well. We like Pierce Whitney and Spencer Thomas. Wesley is one wild card we've bounced around that we both like. We end up hitching it to Charles, and unintentionally give him the same name as the famous hymn composer, Charles Wesley, whose brother, John Wesley, started the Methodist church. When people say we must be good, devout Methodists, I'll have to admit that no, we're just ignorant Presbyterians.

Now as we start to refer to each of them by his or her name, I am beginning to feel them move around from the inside (it's called "quickening"), and it's fun to get to know them in a new way. It's easy to keep track of who is who at this point because no one can wander very far from his or her own placenta and they always stay in the same quadrant of my belly. Pierce, who is breech, is sitting on my left side with his head up under my stomach. Charles is lying sideways across the top, under my diaphragm, his head over Pierce's. Molly is next to Pierce, breech also, on my right side. And Spencer is standing on his head under them all, slightly slanted with his feet kicking Pierce's feet. Molly wakes up and stretches, and in doing so, kicks Spencer, who jerks and wakes up Pierce, who head butts Charles, who wakes up and pushes my diaphragm closer to my throat. My entire body ripples and waves. It is the most amazing thing to feel these people moving around inside of me, independently and interactively. It is so real now. Aliens exist inside of me. I'm never alone. Four others and I are living some kind of crazy, incredible experience like nothing else I'll ever know.

The weeks pass, and I grow. And grow and grow and grow. By the time I am twenty-one weeks, or about five months, my baby bump looks full term to the unsuspecting eye.

With the home monitoring, I—along with my assigned phone nurse in Denver, Linda, who has become an anchor to me and whom I depend on daily to help me maintain my slippery grasp on sanity—continue to track my uterine activity for a full hour at least twice a day to keep a close eye on how many contractions I'm having. When I feel especially crummy, which usually indicates contractions are increasing, or when I notice the actual contractions myself, I strap on the hockey puck sensor for an additional monitoring session. In addition to my required five liters of water a day, if I have more than two contractions in an hour, I have to guzzle a least a liter of water on the spot and re-monitor. If I forget to heat the water enough before drinking it, my temperature drops, my teeth chatter, and I start shaking uncontrollably with chills for several minutes until I warm back up again under blankets and a heating pad. Some days I have only a couple of contractions per hour, and other days, I get way too many, like nearly every five minutes, with a lot of uterine irritability. I chug another liter, then re-monitor. If there is significant improvement, even if I still have one or two over the allowed threshold, it usually means we shouldn't panic and things are getting under control.

It's November 6. I'm pushing fluids to hydrate but it doesn't slow down the contractions. The nurse tells me the time has come for me to go on the drug terbutaline, a medication only approved for lung issues but unofficially used as a tocolytic (a drug that reduces preterm labor). Normally the doctor puts a patient on pills first, but with my precarious situation, Bob doesn't want to mess around with the potentially uneven absorption of oral mediation. A home health nurse comes over to set up a continuous infusion. The medication is delivered via a pump—about the size of a deck of cards—and it will keep a steady flow of the med going through a small tube inserted into the top of my thigh. (It's the same device diabetics use for constant insulin delivery.) I have to muster the courage to ram a needle straight down into my thigh. It takes a little psyching up. I've put a lot of needles into people, but it's different when it's into my own leg.

Whoa. This drug is incredibly annoying. Like every other drug I've used lately, I'm ultra sensitive to terbutaline, and my system overreacts to it. The loading bolus is much more than I can tolerate well. My heartbeat shoots up to a rate double of normal, and my limbs shake with rapid tremors. It makes me nauseated, and I start vomiting again.

I can't sleep. The medication affects the babies too. They're jumping all over the place, probably unable to sleep, shaking, with high heart rates like mine. I hope they aren't throwing up too. As I write in my journal, I can hardly read the words. The whole page is practically illegible. My penmanship looks like a blind ninety-year-old has scratched squiggles on a sheet of paper.

Three days now since the terbutaline began and I've hardly slept. My heart rate is still over 110. The nausea is decreasing a little. But in spite of it all, most importantly, my contractions have slowed down. I've been monitoring a lot more frequently to know how to adjust the medication levels to precisely what they need to be. Each time I monitor and send the data over the phone, my nurse Linda (or whoever is covering her shift when she's off) tells me what to set the pump on. She instructs me to infuse an extra bolus if I have too many contractions or to tweak the hourly infusion rate, to find the lowest effective dose. None of this is very easy. But at least I don't have to go to the hospital. I do *not* want to go to the hospital.

Enjoying the newspaper over breakfast in our little space

CHAPTER 21

THE EXIT PLAN

By night, we slept in Pastor Bates's guest bedroom. We did that for six *months*. By day, we lived in a sort of limbo. I was working the night shift in obstetrics at a hospital forty miles away from the farm. During the day while Jason traded commodities online, I slept on a couch in Jack's office, which often resulted in me being awakened because Jack didn't seem to remember I was sleeping, and he came and went and talked like I wasn't there. Evenings before I went back to work and on my days off, Jason and I labored to make a space in the house's construction zone livable. Though we had to wait on others to do things like order the windows, wire the house, and put in the plumbing, as each thing progressed enough so that we could do our part, we added what we could, like flooring, fixtures, and doors. We stained wood paneling and doors, and painted sheetrock walls. We laid linoleum. I sewed and hung curtains. After half a year, we had two rooms finished enough to live in—bare concrete floors covered by a rug we'd brought from Chicago, and a tiny bathroom with running water and a toilet—but it was our own space to use. We kept frozen icepacks in Aunt Elaine's freezer next door, swapping them out in the cooler we kept in our room to keep milk chilled. Breakfast was cold cereal. Peanut butter sandwiches were for lunch. For dinner we used a microwave to heat up canned pinto beans (or for variety kidney, black, or navy beans) and vegetables. Once a week, we baked muffins at Aunt Elaine's to eat with our legume and broccoli cuisine. (I lost some weight that year.)

During the next six months, with progress slower than crystallized honey in a Minnesota blizzard, I told Jason that I *had* to get out of there. I was going to go crazy. Stark raving mad. And not only would we never overcome our infertility in those circumstances, but we would ruin my relationship with his folks forever if we didn't escape.

We developed an exit plan. We decided I would go back to college where I graduated in Colorado to attend a special program they offered for working RNs to advance their degrees. It was a way to graciously leave Minnesota, with a legitimate reason, without casting blame anywhere. So once again we rented a truck and reloaded our belongings, which were mostly still in boxes in the barn where we'd stacked them the year before. In addition, we rented a trailer to haul the car we'd purchased when we first arrived.

In Colorado Springs, we found a place to live that was perfect for us—a garden apartment in a quadplex. It was a two-bedroom, and it even had a kitchen with a stove. And a refrigerator. What *luxury*. We were delighted to have our very own home again. Outside our back door in the common hallway, there was a washer-dryer hook-up that no one else in the building wanted, so our landlord, Leonard, rented it to us for $20 more a month. The utilities were included in the rent and we paid $345 a month total. How *wonderful* it was.

In no time at all, I found a job with the same hospital I'd worked for when I was a nursing student. The position was a home healthcare nurse in maternal-child care. Day shifts, few weekends, and doing what I loved. Driving from our central office in the morning then going home to home, I visited clients all over town. Wearing my white lab coat and carrying my "doctor" bag, I evaluated and treated patients such as high-risk pregnant women on bed rest, newborn babies with high biliruben under phototherapy, and pediatric patients with things like respiratory illnesses or infections.

Four months after I started the job, winter semester at the university began and I attended my first class in the new program to advance my degree—statistics. But when they handed me the syllabus, and I read through and saw all that math, my stomach flipped. Math is my kryptonite. Math makes my brain bleed, my mind explode. Math is an evil invention that should have been outlawed long ago. And to make things worse that day, the class was occurring at the very hour as my grandfather Russell's funeral that I was missing because of the school's mandatory attendance policy. After scanning the syllabus, it took me about three seconds to decide I wasn't that sold on going back to school after all. Besides, we were out of Minnesota. And I was already doing the nursing job that I wanted to do. I rose from my seat, shuffled out between the row of auditorium seats and students' knees, whispering my apologies to the people still trying to listen to the professor, and I left the classroom for the funeral. Right then and there, furthering my formal, higher education came to an abrupt and unequivocal conclusion.

Also during those first few months after I landed my job, we started to look for a church. This was at a time in my life when I wasn't trusting God farther than I could throw him. I'd walked away from that relationship years earlier. In our first years of marriage, on Sundays if I wasn't at work or sleeping after a Saturday night shift at the hospital, I stayed in bed to read a captivating novel while Jason went to Fourth Presbyterian Church to usher. I had no interest in God. I thought he'd failed me miserably. Nothing about the whole biblical system held an iota of interest for me. If God was going to let me get as hurt as I'd been on his watch, I didn't want anything to do with him. When I'd tossed out that proverbial tub of holy bathwater, I'd thrown out the whole baby with it. And its rubber ducky too. I was done with religion.

Back when I was in college, I'd given nearly all of my time doing "church work." I was a model individual. Quite upright, pious, devout. I was in church every Sunday and several more times a week in organizational or music practice meetings. I went on mission trips. I attended retreats. I had quiet times. I never skipped class, never even thought about smoking or drinking, didn't go anywhere questionable, making sure everything I did was above reproach. I'd kept all of the rules. Never used the words on "The Forbidden Words List" or did things that any church lady could turn her nose up at. When no one else was around to take care of things like leading music or setting up, I did it. When everyone *was* around, I took care of them, making snacks and coffee, cleaning up after meetings, making photocopies and signs, stacking chairs or putting up tables.

A favorite Bible verse was my mantra: Delight thyself in the Lord and he will give you the desires of your heart. I had some pretty specific desires for my future. So I delighted. I delighted like nobody's business. I served joyfully. I worshipped passionately. I gleefully used every free minute I had to work on Christian stuff. I even did some social justice work—not even knowing it was called that—helping a young woman suffering from mental illness and then later during her pregnancy and delivery, advocating for her when the hospital staff treated her poorly because of her demographic.

My selfless work was incessant. But of course, with the Delight Thyself verse as my driving engine, it meant I anticipated a transaction of sorts. While I was busy delighting, I expected God was busy orchestrating circumstances around my life so that I'd get the desires of my heart. If I served him with abandon, then that would seal the deal for me. I wanted my long-term boyfriend to love me and treat me well, as though I was worth something. He'd finally offer me that dreamed-of engagement ring and proposal. Wouldn't that be nice? I so looked forward to that day. And I believed with all my heart it was coming.

But when it didn't, and when it came with a lot more hurt and abandonment, and plenty of damage from those I turned to for help in the midst of my pain, I pulled myself up by my bootstraps and went forward, using a good dose of suppression and denial. And none of that had room for God or any of the unhelpful warped trappings and hypocrisy found within too many churches.

When Jason and I moved to Colorado Springs, we visited my parents' church—the very place I'd sacrificed my life on the altar of busyness and the earning of divine favors—because it was familiar and not too threatening to attend, what with my practiced suppression and denial. Many friendly people, several of whom I already knew, greeted us enthusiastically and included us in their social activities, but they were mostly my parents' age. We needed something different.

Back in the early '80s when I was in nursing school, Tracey, a fellow student, had repeatedly invited me to her church, a newly established group that met in a school cafeteria. "You should come," she said repeatedly. "Come. I think you'll like it." I was so entrenched in my own church group that another congregation held no interest for me. I always declined her invitations. But when Jason and I moved back to town, I remembered Tracey's church and her decade-old unfulfilled invitation, so I suggested to Jason that we check it out. The idea of meeting some people our own age was appealing.

When we arrived, I was off guard, thinking we were just going to mingle, drink coffee, and find some other yuppies to have dinner with. The people were warm and welcoming. Once the service began, they had announcements and a time to visit with people sitting in nearby seats. A small-sized choir sang, the music not overly complex or polished, but the people singing looked like they were enjoying themselves. It contrasted greatly from the sophisticated grand church in Chicago which boasted a paid professional choir, but these people were authentic and kind. We in the congregation sang a few songs together. Someone read something and prayed. And then the sermon began.

The associate pastor, David, was preaching, filling in while the church was between permanent pastors. As David spoke, I felt like the room emptied and David was speaking only to me, telling me that God loved me. It was the most amazing sermon I think I've ever heard. It was as though God was talking directly into my heart, like my heart had ears, and they could hear God tell me he loved me on some incredible spiritual level that only my soul could perceive— like a high-pitched whistle only dogs can hear. As the following week passed, I couldn't wait to get back the next Sunday to hear more. So we returned and once again, I felt like David was speaking just to me, specifically about my own fears and losses, and assuring me that God loved and cared about me. The way those things go, he was probably speaking on Leviticus and how to tell if a cloven-hoofed animal cheweth its cud or not, and the Holy Spirit took the words and transformed them into exactly what I needed to hear. Or maybe not, and everyone in the room heard the same thing. It didn't matter. I was drawn to that place like a magnet. Suddenly, I wanted to go to church. I wanted to hear what David had to say about God. Or what God was going to say into my heart's ears. It was like a light had been turned on in a room I'd closed up and nailed shut to collect spider webs and dead bugs. And when the light came on, it shone amazing truths to me like I'd never known them.

A change began to happen. I started to realize that God's love is real. I didn't know about any of the other stuff. While tossing out the whole bathtub and baby and rubber ducky, I gave up on making sense of the details for the time being. I didn't try to figure out how to work the system, how to understand the rules, or how to grasp what the Bible might truly mean. I just worked from a place of knowing—and *really* knowing because he'd told me—that God loved me.

CHAPTER 22

NOTES ON BEING WHISKED AWAY

I've hit twenty-two weeks! It's a great relief to be able to see the past week in the rearview mirror. I'm doing much better now. My system is finally adjusting to this crazy new drug. Jason set the camera up on the tripod so we can take a picture together, showing off my big belly. This is a huge milestone. The babies are practically viable now, meaning if they are born, they might live.

The pump has been running terbutaline into my leg for seven days now. I'm getting used to my heart galloping at a hundred miles per hour. And the nausea has subsided. I still have the shakes, but not nearly so bad. I don't look so much like a strung-out drug addict needing a fix. What I really want is to go on a walk. These walls are beginning to move in on me, shrinking around me like a haunted house trick room at an amusement park. This apartment is nearly all I've seen for weeks and weeks. But whether I break out or not, I need to keep going, to find a way to not go crazy.

To make sure I don't fry my brain with endless television, I limit myself to a one-hour show in the morning and one other show in the afternoon. The time in between I spend either reading, cross stitching, or writing letters. I allow myself one short nap mid-afternoon. If I slept all day, I'd never get to sleep at night. Just because I'm horizontal it doesn't mean it's okay to float in and out of consciousness. When Jason gets home for the evening, he keeps me company and entertained until bedtime.

A snow storm quilted the landscape outside in fluffy white. I can see the yard is covered through the ground-level living room window, which is fogged up around the edges. It's an old aluminum single-pane window that's a slider and tends to stick. The air is cold right in front of the glass. I've passed from summer to winter barely even knowing the earth has tilted. The trees have changed colors and dropped their leaves without checking with me first. I am twenty-three weeks.

Two days after the snow storm, which is the Sunday before Thanksgiving, Cyndi comes over to trim my hair for me. My thick wavy hair is a long shaggy mess. The style, if you can even call it a style, is way out of fashion, basically like uncut weeds, a grown-out haircut from a past life when I used to go out anytime I wanted. But there isn't anything to be done about it. I can't go to a salon, and we don't have money for it anyway. I mostly need my bangs trimmed so they're out of my eyes. The rest can easily go into a ponytail to stay out of the way.

Somehow as Cyndi is clipping, the scissors fly out of her hand and do cartwheels in midair while she shrieks and slaps the air trying to catch them. Eluding Cyndi's noble effort to snatch them back, the scissors nick me in the eye spinning their way to the floor. Cyndi is devastated for having done this. I try to reassure her and tell her not to worry about it, even as I cup my hand over my weeping eye. I'll be fine.

But when the pain and tearing don't ease up even after a couple of hours, we decide my eye might need to be checked by a professional for a laceration. I call my doctor's answering service, and he returns the call to tell me to go to the ER where they will probably prescribe antibiotic and pain drops, if my cornea does indeed have a gouge in it.

Jason drives me there. After he checks in at the desk with the nurse and lets her know I'm pregnant with quadruplets and on bed rest, she tells me to stay seated in the waiting room and wait until a volunteer comes with a wheelchair to transport me through the security gate and into the ER examination area. The cautious nurse isn't going to take any unnecessary risks with me, which we truly appreciate.

When the exuberant elderly volunteer finally arrives, he quickly helps me get my big body settled into his wheelchair. He's chatty and enthusiastic, all smiles and happy. Once he lowers the drop-down foot rests and I put my feet on them, he takes off, pushing me with plenty of speed. Jason must hustle to keep up with me and my earnest driver. With tears still gushing out of my eye like Niagara Falls, I'm having trouble focusing to see where we are going, but it doesn't take long to realize we've left the waiting room and are heading down the main corridor of the hospital, away from the ER and over to the elevators. Wiping away the tears, I try to look at the volunteer but I can't keep my eyes open for more than two seconds because of the pain, and the water keeps flowing out. I hold a tissue to my cheek, soaking up the salty deluge.

When we stop in front of the elevator doors, the old man gently pats me on the shoulder and sympathetically says, "Don't you worry now. I'm going to get you up to those labor and delivery nurses right away and they'll help you have that baby. Nothing to be upset about."

It takes a second for me to figure out what he's thinking. When it dawns on me, I stifle a chuckle and let him in on the situation.

"No, no. I'm not here to have a baby. I'm having four of them, but not *tonight*. I cut my eye. I just need to get my eye checked so I can go back home and lie down."

Blushing and immediately dropping the nonstop banter, he returns me to the ER and leaves as quickly as possible.

Once I'm checked into an exam room, a doctor puts yellow goo in my eye, dims the overhead lights, and shines a black light in my face. Sure enough, a moon-shaped gouge glows in the ultraviolet light. They give me drops and send me home to go back and resume my bed rest. And to stay away from twirling, flying sharp objects.

CHAPTER 23

THE LUXURIOUS LIFE

Jason's job search in our new town was much more difficult than mine. There were no commercial commodity traders in Colorado Springs. And retail trading was nothing like the work he had done at PaineWebber, or anything remotely like what he wanted to do. It was a good thing our rent was so low. It took Jason ten months to find a job, and then that job only lasted three months. Then a month after it ended, he got a temporary, seasonal job without benefits which ended right before Christmas while I was in the hospital trying not to have babies. That year, our income was about $10,000. The only way we got through it was because of the grocery bags of food left anonymously on our porch, my WIC vouchers, and refraining from doing anything that cost money (except of course seeing doctors who wanted all of our savings).

But remarkably, we weren't terribly stressed. We lived frugally and had what we needed. Our car was paid for and after the previous year, our expectations were relatively simple. I thought our apartment was perfect. We liked the location, the neighborhood, the size, the arrangement with utilities and the laundry. Nothing to complain about.

But I guess I didn't know better.

Once the kids were born and home from the hospital, people started coming over to help with their care. One woman I'd never met before walked into the apartment, took one look around, and said, "Phew, this is small." She made a face and moved around like it might contaminate her.

Another woman came in a few days later and said, "It's so crowded in here. When are you moving?" Not sure what to do with her disapproval, I laughed but assured her we weren't moving. It was what we could afford. It was fine for us. We were fine. Within an hour of her departure that day, her daughter, a realtor, called, saying she'd been referred to us by her mother because we were in the market for a new house, and she wanted to start showing us some properties.

But I *liked* where we lived. No, it wasn't that spacious—only 800 square feet—but not much to clean. None of the babies were ever very far from me, so I could hear each one easily and respond to their needs quickly, always being close by, which was especially helpful at night. When they were drinking enough milk by day to skip their night feeding, we put them in four different cribs so they could fuss without waking each other up. Charlie went in one corner of the apartment in the kitchen eating nook. We turned on the fan above the stove for white noise. Molly slept in the living room across from Charlie with a little black and white TV tuned to an empty channel with static for her white noise. Pierce was in the second bedroom, and Spencer was in our bedroom in a crib pushed into our closet. It worked great. Using pacifiers along with patting and cooing, I had them sleeping mostly all night by the time they were three and a half months old.

Though it was "mostly," I'd hate to mislead anyone and make them think I started getting a lot of sleep then. Figure if a single baby only wakes up one or two nights a week, then you're averaging five nights a week with sleep. Not bad for having a new infant in the house. Add another baby with only one or two bad nights a week, and your average of sleep just went way down. Add two more of them who are in no way trying to coordinate their bad nights with the others, and things look exceedingly more desperate as far as mama-sleep goes. Like I've said before, I'm not any good at math, but I'd say when you add *eight* nights of no sleep in the period of a week (which is *seven* days, mind you), you don't have to be a math wizard to know you're awake more days than exist in a week. It only takes one baby to ruin a night's slumber. Four have a way of making certain you'll never feel rested again.

CHAPTER 24

NOTES ON BEING PARALYZED

Yesterday I turned twenty-five weeks. It's getting so much harder to get up to go to the bathroom. Either the couch is getting a lot deeper or I'm getting a lot bigger. Hmm, I wonder which one it could be. This morning, I'm completing a twenty-four hour monitoring session to see how I'm really doing.

Apparently not so good. While I slept, I had way too many contractions. I can't get them to slow down, in spite of pushing fluids several times, lying on my left side, trying to relax and think positively, and upping the dosage on my little pump. The terbutaline is becoming ineffective, one nurse tells me. She scolds me because I took off the monitor to go to the bathroom. Another nurse tells me to do the opposite of what even another told me. Finally Patty from my obstetrician's office calls and says Dr. Loquacious has decided it's time for me to go to the hospital. As soon as she says it, I burst into tears. The reaction surprises me, since I've been keeping a stiff upper lip and trying to flow with whatever comes up. But now, after I've worked so hard to stay out of the hospital, the emotions suddenly overwhelm me.

While waiting for Jason to come home from work to get me, I have time to reflect on the fortune of lasting at home as long as I have. I'd hoped to stay until Thanksgiving, and we've passed that goal by a week and a day. The tearful sadness is replaced by gratitude for that fact. When Jason arrives, we pack a small suitcase, and I look around a last time knowing the next time I see our apartment, come what may, I will not be the same. We go to the hospital and as the doctor foretold, the doors shut behind me not to be exited again until one way or the other I have delivered four babies.

They admit me into one of their four intensive care antepartum rooms. I have bathroom privileges, which means I don't have to use a bedpan (yay). With the amount of water I drink, this is a huge deal. My room is private, so I don't have a roommate (another yay), and all of the nurses are caring and helpful. With the controlled environment, my contractions slow enough that the worries of home management are relieved.

That is, for two days anyway.

Then I break through the terbutaline, and my contractions go out of control. My heart rate is too high, so we can't increase the terbutaline any more. The time is here to try a new medication, an IV drug called magnesium sulfate, a central nervous system depressant. But like all the other medications I've taken, this drug is stronger with more side effects than I can tolerate.

The loading dose paralyzes me. I can't lift my arms or legs, and I can't even move my mouth to talk right. My slurred speech around my thick tongue is like a slowed, warped record album and no one can understand me. The med does a number on my sinuses too. They've swollen shut, and I can only breathe through my mouth, which is completely dried out. My tongue is glued to the roof of my mouth, and my lips are swollen, cracked, and unbearable. They won't let me drink anything, and they've taken away my water pitcher because my fluid balance is totally screwed up and I have fluid overload. They're worried more water will drown my lungs and stress my heart too much.

My skin is burning, a searing heat coming from deep inside of me—like the worst unending hot flash the world ever created—and my nerves have gone haywire. It feels like my skin is crawling off my body, like thousands of bugs are under my skin and they're digging their way out. I can't do a lick about any of this because I can't move, I can't speak, I can't even moan well. They've mounted a stuffy oxygen mask over my face because I'm not breathing enough, and they put in a urinary catheter too. But I'm too absolutely, tortuously wretched to even care. This is like death, I think. Except with death, there would be an end to the suffering.

The only relief, as slight as it is, comes from the window of my hospital room. After plenty of slurred mumbling from me, someone finally understands and opens the window. December snow flurries are blustering in, lifting and billowing the curtains. The sweet cold air is blowing over my fiery skin as I lie unmoving on top of my bed. All the nurses who come in wear their puffy winter coats, trying to keep warm as they care for me. They don't stay very long, rubbing their hands between tasks and hugging themselves when they hurry back out. My family members sit next to my bedside shivering, at a loss for how to help me. I try to form the words to ask somebody, anybody, to get the sheet off me or to move my top leg off the other one where my knobby knee is pressing painfully into the other leg. If someone could just press their palms against my legs, it would help a little to keep my skin from crawling off my muscles. When I finally fall asleep for a few minutes and find momentary relief, I wake up with alarms blaring because I've stopped breathing and the oxygen level in my blood has dropped too much. I am short of breath and my chest aches.

My pulse is racing once more from the terbutaline, which they are trying to use again because the mag sulfate has paralyzed me and they have to back it off. I'm beginning to have cardiac arrhythmias. And none of this is stopping my labor. My contractions are coming every three minutes. With each contraction, it feels as though a blood pressure cuff is inflating around my neck, increasing the pressure in my chest, neck, and head so much that I can't breathe. I'm certain I'm going to have a stroke and afraid my head is literally going to explode. Too unstable to be moved from the high-risk obstetrical unit to the Cardiac ICU, they connect me by a remote hookup to telemetry in the specialized cardiac wing where a technician sits at a desk staring at my readout, constantly monitoring my heart.

In the meantime, my doctors are coming to the conclusion that it will be too risky to my health to continue trying to keep our babies from being born. My body can't take any more of this.

Through the fog of medication and physical agony, I realize Bob is standing at my bedside sadly explaining to me there is nothing more he can do, that my body and heart can't tolerate any more of this. He tells Jason and me they are stopping all the tocolytic drugs and must give up trying to delay the delivery. We have to let the babies come. There is no other option. He is ordering a shot of Demerol to sedate me to try to make me more comfortable. We will have to brace ourselves and deal with what comes, and expect that the birth is imminent. The NICU is put on high alert. The OR staff is on stand-by. We must prepare to have four babies fourteen weeks early.

Stunned and frightened, my extended family who have been watching and listening to my doctors and nurses from the corners of the room, silently slip out to go home to bed, to pray, and await news. Although Jason has been going home every night—something we agreed he would do when I entered the hospital this time since I could be here a very long time—he stays in my room this night, sitting in the chair next to my bed. After they give me the shot of Demerol, I feel the chemical relief growing and seeping into my bloodstream and, mercifully, I lapse into a drugged sleep where for a time, I finally get relief from the myriad of horrible physical sensations that I can barely take for even one more second.

CHAPTER 25

THE WAKE-UP CALL

Jason and I attended the wedding of a friend I'd known in college. During the reception, we ran into another old friend of mine, Marsha, whom I hadn't seen for ages. When I was in high school, she'd taken violin lessons from my dad. Every time I see her she fondly recalls when I'd helped her drive in snow for the first time. She'd called in a bit of a panic, needing to come to my house for her scheduled lesson. Having recently moved from California to Colorado, she had never driven on icy roads before. Over the phone, I described to her how to maneuver the car when she hit something slick, how to pump the brakes, and how to steer into a slide. That day she made it safely to her lesson and said she always remembered my assurances that she could do it.

At the wedding reception, Marsha and I were catching up over pieces of wedding cake and coffee, updating each other about our families since we'd seen each other last, which had been long before I had the kids. Then she told me a fascinating story.

In the middle of one night, she said that God woke her from a sound sleep and told her to pray for me. She didn't know what was going on or what to pray for exactly, but by golly, if God was going to yank her out from a sound sleep in the middle of the night and tell her to pray for me, she was going to do it.

She explained what details she remembered of when it happened and what she learned about me after the fact, like that I was in the hospital and how long I'd been in. From everything we could figure, the night God woke her up was the very night I was having the terrible complications and the doctors gave up saving the pregnancy. My eyes welled with tears as we realized she had prayed with us through that precarious night when I was about to deliver our micro premie babies.

Her story taught me some important things about God, whom I was getting to know more authentically for the first time. One thing, he likes to involve people in the projects he's working on. I guess he could wave a wand and make things happen, but where's the fun in that? You might get more sleep, but you'd miss out on the excitement. How much more meaningful is it to be a part of the adventure, plus develop relationships in the process? We thrive so much better in a community relating to others, sharing life together.

Secondly, I learned that God doesn't always explain himself. (Isn't that an understatement?) Needless to say, most things don't make sense to us. *Why this?* or *how come that?* we wonder. We see things only "through a glass darkly." But the being who said, "Let there be…" and the universe banged into existence, is too huge for our limited human brains to comprehend and figure out. Who'd want to worship a god as ordinary as ourselves, a god we could predict, explain, and know all about? To me, that's too small of a deity. I'd rather go with the one who is too big to grasp. And with that, comes a God who will wake up a friend out of a restful sleep to take part in a pretty spectacular adventure.

CHAPTER 26

NOTES ON BEING RESCUED

Sunlight coming in through my window rouses me from a deep sleep. I blink a few times to come fully awake and realize where I am. Oh, yes. In the hospital. And everything was going wrong last night. I realize this was the best night's sleep I've had for longer than I can remember. My pain is diminished to a tolerable level. I can't feel any perceivable contractions, and certainly not the kind that were strangling me and making my head nearly explode. My heartbeat feels like it has returned to a regular rhythm and slowed down to a livable speed. And more than anything, our babies are still inside of me!

My obstetrician examines me to assess my condition. Even after contracting every three minutes, I've had no cervical changes. Unimaginable. On telemetry, my heart is beating like it should, the right speed without arrhythmias.

With everything stable and steady again, they ease me back onto the terbutaline which might buy our tiny babies more time, as long as I tolerate it. They keep me connected to the telemetry, the data being constantly transmitted to the Cardiac Care Unit, to make sure my heart is okay as the terbutaline is ticked back up. They also put me on incredibly high doses of Motrin, which some studies have indicated might reduce preterm labor. But we have to be extremely cautious, with daily biophysical ultrasounds to make sure the babies are tolerating it. The unprecedented dose can cause kidney problems for them.

I've made it to twenty-six weeks. Because everything has stabilized and seems less precarious for now, they remove the tubes they'd put into me, and I can get up and have the first shower I've had in a week. The cool water on my itchy scalp is a balm. To be clean goes a long way to making me feel like I can cope. One of my wonderful nurses says she'll shave my legs if I can get my hands on an electric razor. I happen to have a Lady Remington at home—a shared Christmas present from our teen years that my sisters bequeathed to me when we all moved out of our parents' house. Jason brings it. Showered and shampooed and shaved, I feel human again.

When Jason came to spend the evening with me, he parked the car on the street in the neighborhood near the hospital like he usually must do because the hospital parking garage is always packed and he can never find a spot. When he left to go home at about ten o'clock, it was dark and hard to see. As he pulled away from the curb wondering why it was so cold and loud, he looked into the rearview mirror when a street light illuminated the back window. Or where the window should have been. Instead he saw the glimmering bits of shattered glass all over the backseat of the car. Someone had smashed out the rear window. Our insurance deductable is about the cost of a new window, so we'll have to pay out-of-pocket and try not to be bitter about the stranger out there who caused us this unneeded bad luck.

Things on the baby front are momentarily staying quiet. The main problem is from the Motrin. Spencer's amniotic fluid is decreasing, which means he's starting to have renal impact. By Thursday, when I reach twenty-seven weeks, we have to discontinue the Motrin. Then they continue to closely monitor Spencer afterwards, to make sure he recovers. After a few days, his fluid level starts to improve. The doctor is still watching him extra closely even so because he's falling behind the others in size and weight and becoming more at risk for complications.

Six days before Christmas, it's Saturday, and once again Jason is laid off from work. Oh, well. Who needs an income anyway? We have already figured out how to do without groceries for the most part. Every morning for breakfast before work, Jason has a bowl of cereal. (Don't tell anyone, but it might be some of my WIC cereal and milk that was left over when I came into the hospital. *Maybe.*) And for lunch at work, he's been having a peanut butter sandwich. (Again, maybe it might have some WIC ingredients.) Then for supper, he comes to the hospital to spend the evening with me. Each morning, I've perused my daily hospital cafeteria menu like I'm eating at a fine restaurant to choose what magnificent gourmet meal I think Jason will enjoy. I circle my choices with the supplied golf pencil, plus—here's the key—I also indicate I'd like to have the largest of the three portion sizes they offer. Then when supper is served, I eat a few bites and have to stop because squeezing in even a little bit of food is more expansion than I can tolerate without triggering new pain. What remains on my plate Jason gets to eat. On weekends, he's been foregoing the lunch PB&J and having hospital gourmet *twice* in one day. Oh, boy.

The Saturday he is laid off, my doctor decides to make it a better day for us. He is sending us on a date. Just a hospital date, but still. You work with what you've got, do the best you can. Even though he's issued a pass for me to leave my room for an outing, I can't go any farther than the cafeteria. And I have to go there in a wheelchair. But who cares? Eating cuisine *à l'hospital* is so much better sitting up, seeing out a different window, eating at a table. It's divine. I dress in regular clothes, which I try to do on the days I don't feel too bad or am not paralyzed, because it's a lot better not to spend so many months in a hospital gown. Staying in your pajamas for weeks on end can make you feel like you're sick or something. Real clothes help make me feel normal, even if the clothes are huge and more like spandex tents.

After our date downstairs, Jason wheels me back to my room. My nurses have set up a VCR they found in some conference room, and they've rounded up a VHS of *Memoirs of an Invisible Man*. Jason crawls up onto the bed next to me, and we settle in for the picture show. For a short time I almost forget I'm in the hospital.

For the following days, it is unquestioningly a boon to have Jason with me full time as the holidays approach. We don't worry too much about his lack of employment. Worry won't change anything, will it? And word is, Current might rehire him after the new year when business picks up again for the coming Valentine season.

A friend brought me Chinese carry out from the Imperial Wok restaurant for lunch today. I *love* sweet and sour pork. And egg rolls! A delightful, welcome change. And thank God I'm doing well enough to visit with her and eat normal food. I'd awakened at a quarter till four in the morning with way too many contractions yesterday. I almost had to go back on mag sulfate.

Another ultrasound shows Spencer's amniotic fluid level is continuing to increase. Charlie and Molly are both about two pounds, two ounces. Pierce measured as smaller than two pounds, which is different enough from before (when he'd become the biggest) that Bob doesn't think the measurement is accurate this scan. Spencer is only one pound, twelve ounces, and we believe that estimate because he's always been the smallest. They're watching him closely for distress. If he becomes too compromised, then that's all she wrote. They'll have to deliver them all.

Christmas Eve comes and I get a phone call that my grandmother Nora (my mom's mom) has died. It's eleven months since that day in statistics when I bailed and went to my mom's dad's funeral. Because I can only go as far as the cafeteria in a wheelchair, I won't be going to the funeral, which will probably be in Denver, over an hour away by car. (A lot farther by wheelchair.) She's been in poor health in a nursing home for quite a while, so it isn't completely an unexpected thing, but still. Even so, I will try not to dwell on it. I need to think of happy things, to stay positive for the babies. So what should I ponder?

Christmas is coming. With no chimney in my room, I know Santa won't be coming in person to visit in the night, but I can find reasons to be cheerful and celebrate. I am still pregnant this far into our adventure and for the most part, the babies are looking healthy. And as a bonus, I get to have Jason with me every day, now that he is unemployed. There isn't any need to fret. All is well.

It's Christmas! Since I'm relatively stable, I score another pass from the doctor to leave my room for lunch. Jason wheels me back to the hospital cafeteria for a half-hour to enjoy a Christmas dinner served on an institutional heavy ceramic plate in the center of a fiberglass orange tray. The holiday fare includes pressed turkey fabrication wrapped around mushy stuff (not to be confused with dressing), plus a few other overcooked sides. I find it altogether yummy.

After lunch when I'm settled back into my bed, family members start coming to visit bearing gifts and holiday wishes. Cyndi arrives first. She gives us beautiful quilts she's handmade for each of the babies. Each is made in a different color theme: pink, blue, green, and purple. My room is decorated for the holiday because of Cyndi. Last week she brought in Christmas decorations, and she and Jason put them up. They hung twinkling lights around my bulletin board where our greeting cards are on display, draped garlands along the window curtains, and hung ornaments from any spot that would hold them. They transformed my hospital room into a festive party place. Bows and ribbons and bulbs dangle from my TV and I have a miniature Christmas tree the size of a milk carton. The scarlet poinsettia plant and beribboned bouquet of Christmas carnations are beautiful.

Next, my teenage sister, Colleen, arrives with my parents' high school foreign exchange student who has brought us a beautiful, delicate glass world globe ornament with a mark on the country of Germany to indicate her home town of Berlin. Colleen brings four large wrapped bundles, and inside are the softest teddy bears I've ever touched. Three brown and one white.

After they leave, my parents come. They stay for a short visit, then leave to go find dinner. They're coming back after they eat. Cyndi returns for a while, and then by evening Suzy, the sister between Cyndi and me, comes from Texas with her husband. She gives me...hold onto your hat...a roll of toilet paper.

This is very odd. It isn't even wrapped in Christmas paper. I don't understand. But she has a delightful glint in her eye.

Am I missing something? She prompts me with her elfish grin to hurry up and unroll it. Within the first few squares I find...*money*. Taped along the length of the toilet paper is a dollar bill. I look up at her with my eyebrows raised.

"Keep going," she says with a huge smile.

I unwind some more. Another bill. And another. Fives, tens, twenties are taped inside the roll. I'm unrolling lots and lots of money.

"It's a diaper fund!" she crows. "I started a diaper fund at work." (She works at the law firm in Texas that helped us with our insurance woes.) "Everyone is helping. I get snacks and drinks at Sam's and sell them in the break room."

The roll of toilet paper keeps going for yards and yards. This first installment has nearly $200 in it!

"Everyone knows about you. Some people just walk by and toss money into the jar without buying anything." She is loving this. So am I. I'm overwhelmed with gratitude. I'm touched that so many people—people I've never met—are rallying around us like this. And that my sister is doing so much to provide for such a basic necessity.

Jason drapes the unrolled ribbon of money over his shoulders and chest and I take a picture to commemorate it. Though an unusual experience to have Christmas while in the hospital, this has been a lovely day. Full of love, care, and fun.

The next day, my grandpa—my dad's dad—comes from Denver to see me. I don't know what my dad did to convince him to come. I am touched he did. Since Grandma died over five years ago, he rarely leaves his house, let alone Denver. He never wanders farther than the KFC or McDonald's or his bank, all within a couple blocks of his house. It is a delight to get to see him and visit for a while. He gives us $100, which is an incredible windfall for us. That, with what Suzy gave us, is more cash than we've held in our hands for a long time.

My brother and his family also visit from Denver, following on Grandpa's heels. They come bearing gifts too. They give me this huge, bulky package. Inside are giant furry Mallard duck slippers. I love Mallard ducks. These are delightful and incredibly fun, the kind of gift that isn't given because it's especially useful but because of the smiles and laughter it brings. What a special day this has been.

CHAPTER 27

THE NEW HOUSE

I was completely happy with our snug little apartment. Truly. At least I was until the Great Ant Invasion. And until Leonard, our 83-year-old landlord, sold the quadplex and the new management raised our rent. *And* made us start paying utilities separately on top of the higher rent. And a couch surfer moved in upstairs with our neighbor and spent his jobless days working on his old clunker van, the engine revving and spewing black stinky exhaust at all hours two feet outside our garden-level bedroom window. I couldn't count the number of times he woke me up. And the choking *stench*. It was hard to breathe. I wanted to scream. Or take a sledge hammer to his stupid junk heap of a car.

And yes, I was honestly content with our snug little apartment until our four tiny premie babies grew into not-so-tiny active tots who stopped lying right where I put them—with a couple of them even trying to *walk*.

When they were still infants, the first time Leonard saw them was the day he dropped by the apartment complex when we were unloading them from the car at the back door. Our first infant car seats (rented from the hospital for a year at just $5 each) did not have carry handles, so we had to use both hands to carry one at a time. That made loading the car for outings a bit tricky, especially when they were still on oxygen and monitors with extra equipment to haul. We had to do a "fox, chicken, bag of grain across the road" kind of maneuver to get them into the car. To not leave any of them unattended, we actually needed three adults to get all four of them from inside the apartment into the car, but if we hustled, we could do it with two of us—if Child Protective Services or kidnappers weren't around to see us leave any of them alone in the car when we dashed inside for the next one.

The day Leonard came, we'd just started the fox-chicken-grain maneuver. We introduced him to our quadruplets, and he was mightily impressed with Jason and his manliness at being able to produce four children at once. He went on and on about it, expressing his amazement at the amount of testosterone it must have taken. (I refrained from telling Leonard the reason we had four was because of the exact opposite of fertility prowess.) Unfortunately, his excitement about our four babies didn't last. By the time he was selling the place, he was angry at us and said it wasn't in our lease that we could add four more people. He didn't like that we kept the thermostat warm enough for the kids. He didn't appreciate working around our scheduled naps to come in to re-grout the bathtub and paint the living room. He was under a lot of stress, trying to get the property ready to show and sell while working with his ex-wife and her new husband who co-owned it with him. It wasn't going very smoothly. And he didn't appreciate that we didn't want ants everywhere. As the kids lay on the living room floor, a migration of hundreds of ants marched southwest across the room, streaming up and over the lumps of children in their way. The ant trap Leonard put outside didn't work, and an exterminator said Leonard needed to fix the crack in the foundation to keep the insects out. I think Leonard saw us as "high maintenance," and he just wanted to be out of the rental business.

The ants, the increased cost, and the shrinking space as the kids grew triggered the realization that we might want to consider other options if we could find an alternative we could afford.

We began looking at houses in our price bracket. I had a wish list for my dream house and hoped that maybe we could find something with one or maybe even two of the features. My ultimate fantasy home would include a yard for the kids to play in and maybe even a garden. And a fence around said idyllic yard would be a huge plus so I wouldn't always have to be right there once they got older. I'd love a garage so Jason wouldn't have to scrape ice off the windshield on winter mornings or fret about hail damage to the car every summer storm. And what if we had a bedroom for each kid—that felt a bit over the top, but hey, what's life without dreams? A recreation room or someplace for them to play inside would be fantastic, and maybe more than one bathroom would come in handy, especially once they were teenagers. But no matter what our realtor showed us, everything we saw was a dump— shoeboxes with holes in the walls, stained carpets, broken doors. No house we saw was anything *close* to what would work or what we'd hoped for.

Then finally, one day we found one that could work. It was fairly small but in much better repair then anything else we'd seen. If we tried hard enough, we could get excited about it. With our realtor, we prepared the paperwork and submitted an offer. We waited expectantly for the phone to ring after we knew our realtor had contacted the sellers. When the phone rang, our hearts sped up. But his hello was not encouraging. Someone else had swept in about the same time we made our offer and they also put in a bid. And they offered to buy it with *cash*. We were out of luck. They took the cash. We took a hiatus. We needed a break from looking to regroup and think again. We revisited our finances, found one retirement fund left from our Chicago days that we could raid for the price of a hefty fine, and after some reworking, we applied and pre-qualified for a special kind of loan that gave us an especially low interest rate that would keep our mortgage almost the same as our rent. With this new loan, we were able to increase our price range by another ten grand.

With a new list of houses on his clipboard, our realtor took us out again. We walked into our future house with our jaws hanging open. We asked the realtor to recheck his notes, was it truly the price he'd quoted? It was a beautiful ranch with a finished basement that included a huge rec room and a laundry room just as big. Three bedrooms upstairs and two downstairs. A garage, a yard, a fence, and *three* bathrooms. The owner was a handyman, so there were a lot of extras like hardwood trim everywhere and built-in oak shelves. Certain the moment another realtor showed it, it would be gone, we put in an offer immediately. And the sellers accepted!

A month later at the closing, we sat around a long table in a conference room, each of us with our complimentary bottle of water and company pen. The title company administrator had a tall pile of documents for us to sign, and then the house would be ours. But before we began, the sellers asked us for the second time that week if we'd be willing to postpone. They didn't have anywhere arranged to move. They hadn't truly thought they'd sell it and didn't have a backup plan yet. They'd put it on the market without really knowing why or thinking it through. We felt bad for them—honestly—but we couldn't postpone. Our notice was turned in at our apartment, and the new management was giving us grief as it was. We had the truck reserved, the movers lined up, and nowhere else to live. We just couldn't. They were baffled that the sale was occurring but went ahead and signed everything and turned over the keys. In a snow storm the day before Christmas Eve, we moved into our dream house, a month before the kids turned one year old. (And the sellers moved into an apartment somewhere else in town and began plans to have a new house built for themselves.)

After the fact, as I reflected about how ideal the house was for us—undoubtedly a tremendous gift—I think I figured out why the owners sold it without thinking. Who knows? But I can't help but believe there were unseen powers at work, greater than any of us, that knew how perfect that house was for our family, and that we really needed to have it. Whatever the reason though, I am grateful.

CHAPTER 28

NOTES ON BEING BEYOND CHALLENGED

I must have had too much fun over the Christmas weekend because by Monday I feel awful. Whenever my contractions are increasing, even if I cannot perceive them, I feel lousy. Or maybe it's that whenever I feel lousy my contractions increase. The chicken-egg egg-chicken thing. Again, my caretakers are weighing the idea of putting me back on magnesium sulfate, which is almost the last thing I want to do. I am nearly ready to give up and quit trying. I'm so weary, worn out, used up, and depleted. The idea of throwing in the towel is seducing me, tempting me to choose the exit that will let me get off this difficult ride.

For a distraction, I pull out some reading material to flip through, though I'm really using the time to decide if I am going to surrender my resolve. Suzy and her husband Steve paid the fee for me so I could join a group called The Triplet Connection, a support and informational group for larger multiples. (That would be larger quantities, not larger babies.) They publish a periodical with tips and support for those having triplets, plus a few things about quads and quints. I peruse one of their issues, hoping to get through a few more minutes before I…what? I don't know what I'll do. So much of this whole journey is willpower. The will to keep going, to keep a positive outlook, to keep hope alive. Among many features, *The Triplet Connection* magazine has an entire section devoted to memorials to babies who didn't survive. I read about triplets and quadruplets born at 18 weeks, 24 weeks, 30 weeks. Some or all of them died. This re-awakes me to the reality of things. I *can't* give up yet. My babies could *die*. Or they could be damaged for *life* if they come too soon. It's not that difficult to know what I must do. Once again I become determined to go for the long haul and keep my babies inside me even longer. No matter how hard it is.

It is amazing how much mental attitude impacts my condition. But then there are times that my mindset seems to have little to do with what is happening inside of me. Or maybe it's so subtle what is going on that I can't recognize the emotional toll something takes on my psyche and how it lowers my threshold for tolerance for even the smallest stimulation. Some days I can't even have a visitor in my room because the provocation makes my contractions pick up in frequency.

A woman I knew in college comes to visit me unannounced. I'd helped her when she had an unexpected pregnancy and needed support my senior year of nursing school. Needing a subject for my obstetrical unit project, I asked her if I could work with her during her pregnancy on nutrition and exercise and write a paper about the process. She agreed, and we became friends. I was even her Lamaze partner and was with her for the delivery. I also was the one whom she'd call at midnight to come pick her up when she found herself in compromising situations and needed a ride home. I came to learn over time that she suffered from mental illness and was a tough friend to have. Ten years later I ran into her when she was in my hospital having her second baby when I was working as a homecare nurse. Because of the reconnection, she called me later when I was home on bed rest and wanted me to help her sister who is a brittle diabetic and pregnant, against her doctor's advice. I explained to her that I wasn't in a position to be able to help since I was trying to keep my own pregnancy safe. I gave her some names and agencies she could call to inquire about support for her sister. So it is quite a surprise when she shows up in my hospital room. She has her toddler with her, plus her mother and her pregnant sister. She wants me—from my hospital bed—to counsel and help her sister. While I try to manage the conversation and politely decline, attempting to redirect them away from my orbit, her toddler runs around the room, pulling my things off the shelves, turning knobs, pushing buttons, and pretty much exemplifying entropy. Normally, I realize kids can be noisy and active and that is fine, but in these circumstances, it does me no favors. My contractions start spiking as the stress in the room swells. I need her to leave and to quit demanding things of me. She dashes out for a few minutes to chase her escaped son down the hallway, so I quickly thank her mom and sister for coming to visit me, and I wish them a good day.

They don't leave. They simply stare at me in awkward silence, shifting their weight from one foot to the other, waiting for me to guide the conversation to its next phase. What more can I say to convey I *cannot* help them? That they need to *go away*. I can only hope they will realize this is a strange and uncomfortable encounter, and that they never should have come.

The woman and her son come back and pick up right where we'd left off, the little monster, er, ah, boy ransacking my tapes and tape player. With a desperate effort, I say as bluntly as possible that I can't help them. She doesn't give up easily and presses further. I tell her again to call social services. I'm depleted and have nothing more to give. Finally they leave. I call my nurse, and she does what she can to get my contractions back under control. She also adds a notice on the door that says all visitors must check in at the nurses' station before entering my room. I breathe a sigh of relief. Hopefully that will keep out future stresses and unwelcomed intrusions. I've got to keep my babies safe.

But the notice on the door can't protect me from the Pink Ladies. They breach the blockade with brazen nonchalance.

Word has spread among the mostly-senior volunteer ladies who take the book carts from room to room and do things to help patients be more comfortable. They've heard there's a pregnant woman expecting quadruplets in the hospital. Many of them apparently want to have a look at me for themselves. Some at least feign legitimate reasons for coming into my room, like to offer a magazine or see if they can refill my water pitcher. Others come in and simply say they know someone who knows someone who knows me. But every single one of them who comes in checks me out and tries to see how big I am. One even says, "You're not that big," kind of smugly, like she proved me to be a fraud. Thing is, she is comparing me to how a full-term woman looks who comes to the hospital ready to have her baby. She isn't considering I am only six months along looking like I am ten. Plus, I am lying in bed surrounded by pillows. Besides, who says it is a competition? *Sheez*.

One day I am having an ultrasound so I am mostly naked, my huge, tight round belly completely exposed and I'm wearing just a bra with a towel over my lap. A Pink Lady comes into my room, whips back the curtain, and barges in. My nurse Maggie throws her body over mine, bracing her hands on my pillow on either side of my head to make a tent with her torso, trying to protect my privacy and dignity.

"We're having an ultrasound here," she protests to the intruder as she shields me from the prying eyes.

Standing tall and undaunted, the Pink Lady says, "I have a friend who knows your parents, so I wanted to come introduce myself."

Maggie exclaims, "This isn't a good time!"

The Pink Lady says, "Oh, I'll only stay five minutes."

Nuh-uh.

Maggie kicks her out.

Afterwards, the head nurse of Labor and Delivery apologizes to me, meets with the coordinator of the Pink Ladies, and forbids them from intruding on me anymore. She adds emphasis to the note on the door that *everyone* must check in before opening my door. (Well, Jason doesn't have to.) After that, things are much more peaceful and controlled, and no one else who knows someone who knows someone who once stood next to my mother in a church pew comes in to gawk at me and challenge me for not being as big as they think I should be or demand that I help them fix their sister's high-risk pregnancy.

A few things happen while I'm incubating, waiting, trying to hang on as long as I possibly can. Cyndi donates blood for me in case I need a transfusion when I have my Cesarean. We both have B-positive blood. The donation wipes her out, and it takes her a long time to recover and feel well again. Her gift is quite a sacrifice, and I so appreciate it. Also, on an unseasonably balmy day, Jason gets permission to take me outside in a wheelchair. He pushes me along the sidewalk around the park next to the hospital, and it's like going to heaven, it's so nice to be outside. Lots of people are in the park too, enjoying the warmth and sunshine, and I feel like I've rejoined the human race. And a final development is—which is essential and a huge checkmark on our "to do" list—I engage a doctor to be our pediatrician. A while ago I called around to pediatric practices to find a doctor who is taking new patients, and one who would accept Medicaid patients. One of the doctors whose practice I called comes into my room so I can interview him and see if I'll use him. I ask all kinds of questions, like what is his experience with NICU babies (he had a special rotation in NICU during his residency) and how would he coordinate care with a neonatologist when they share responsibility in the NICU? He has all the right answers, so I am happy to sign him on to be my babies' doctor. It's unexpected and more than a little surprising that he is so willing to accommodate me, coming to my hospital room, letting me interrogate him thoroughly, and vying eagerly for the position. He seems to want this job badly. I find out that one of the other doctors in his practice is the pediatrician for my friend's quadruplets (the two girls and two boys), and the partner likes to boast about being their doctor. Now my new pediatrician will have ammunition to fire back because he'll have his own set of quadruplets. *So there.*

Now with Christmas over, having decided I will remain pregnant a while longer, I need something to do to keep calm, and also busy to keep my mind too occupied to go crazy. I've found a new project, one that will pass the time and encourage me to keep on keeping on.

Throughout the Christmas season, greeting cards poured into our mailbox. They were filled with good tidings for the holidays and news that people from all over the country are praying for us and the babies. Some of these are from new friends we've never even met. They know someone who knows someone, or they heard of us through the grapevine or a prayer chain. Though many are strangers to us, I believe all these faithful people are a huge part of the reason I didn't deliver that night the doctors had to give up. Wanting to put those beautiful cards to good use and to continue enjoying them and their colorful pictures, glitter, and gloss, I have an inspired idea and know what I want to do.

Using a pencil at first to make guidelines, I draw big boxy numbers on the pretty front panels of the largest cards, utilizing as much of the surface area as possible. With my tongue out and anchored at the corner of my mouth (where I've always stuck it when I'm concentrating on a project) and with a sharp pair of scissors, I begin cutting the cards into giant numbers. I start with the number twenty-eight, the week of pregnancy we're on right now. It's a red and gold embossed number "2" that's seven inches tall, plus an "8" out of glossy green, gold, and red plaid. Out of a smaller card with a nativity scene I cut a plus sign. After that, starting first with a royal blue satin card, I make a "1" through "6," which will count the days leading up to my next week of the pregnancy.

Before Jason goes home for the night, we implement what we're developing as our new ritual. He hangs up the appropriate number to mark what day of the pregnancy we are on and to show we have made it through another day without delivering. It is much nicer to count forward, enjoying each day we successfully endure, instead of picking out some arbitrary date in the future and checking off days to countdown toward the goal, hoping to get there but knowing we might not. That's just setting us up for failure.

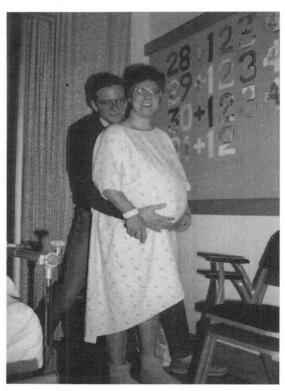

It's taking several days to cut up all of our cards. After a while and some practice, I don't need to pencil them in first anymore and I snip away, freewheeling it. I have quite a pile of numbers. We're going to persevere a long time, if the quantity I've cut out is any indication. I'm very optimistic now. It's a great project for me. Even when I'm worn out on this pregnancy thing and am tempted to give up, I will remember the numbers and how much I want to hang up another set.

My ribs are beginning to spread apart so fast to accommodate these alien life forms growing inside of me that my intercostal muscles—those are the ones between the ribs that on a pig are called a rack and you eat them with dripping barbecue sauce—are spasming and making it hard to lie here without squirming and moaning every few minutes. My pelvis and hips are having quite a hard time too. Guess they're not really designed to spread so wide like a butterfly's wings. They are not happy. A couple times a day my physical therapists pack my torso in hot compresses and give me massages to try to ease the spasms. A couple of times I have soaked in a Jacuzzi they have here for water births, trying to ease the muscle pain. The water can't be too hot but still it feels so good. It is an exhausting activity, but it helps to relieve the discomfort for a while. My therapists also get approval to put me in a new bed because I am developing bed sores. It's a special air fluidized bed (often used for paralyzed people) that keeps me suspended on a mattress of air. The skin on my hips is sore, red, and is starting to break down—a serious complication for bedridden people. When I need to get up on the days they still let me use the commode chair next to the bed, someone switches off the bed to stop my levitation, and the surface sinks down so that my feet descend until they're low enough to touch the tile. When I get back in, I sit on the edge and lie back sideways. Someone hits the switch, and the air rushes back into the mattress to elevate me into the air again. As much work as it is to get in and out of the special bed, it's helping to relieve the pressure sores on my body. My therapists say my hips are looking a little better. I can't actually see them, so I'll take their word for it. And I'm glad to hear it's working because the bed costs about a thousand dollars a day.

For lunch, I make the mistake of eating three bites of food instead of two, my usual limit, and now the pain and pressure are sudden and tremendous. One stupid bite sends me into intractable misery, like I've swallowed a tiny sponge capsule that expands into a dinosaur inside of me in three seconds flat. Sometimes I forget to count bites, or something tastes good and I simply stick another bite in because my life is a little dull and weird right now. But then *whammy.* The dinosaur inflates.

I feel wretched. This hurts so bad. Everything is getting so hard. Eating, lying, turning, breathing. When I can't take another minute facing the wall on this side because my hip, ribs, and side ache so much I can concentrate on nothing else, I must turn onto my other side. Struggling like a turtle on its back to roll the other way flattens me onto my back on the way over. I'm tempted to stop here. It hurts less. It's such a relief to be supine. But for like only two seconds, because while I'm completely flat, even for only a couple of blinks, my vision narrows and spots spark in the closing darkness. The weight of four babies and four placentas crushes my aorta and cuts off the blood flow to everywhere—like my brain, for example. I need to finish the turn and get back onto my side.

Even with my fancy cut-out numbers to hang up on the wall, I don't know how much longer I can do this. Some moments I'm so ready to knuckle under, it's all I can do to keep going. Minute by minute I've got to muster as much mental discipline as I can to keep going, psyche myself up again, remember why I'm doing this, remind myself of what can happen if I don't keep them inside longer. But I don't know if I have what it takes to do this. This. Is. So. Hard. I'm crying because they've told me my contractions are breaking through and I am probably going to have to go back on that nasty, horrible, tortuous magnesium sulfate. I can't be strong right now. I'm pathetic. The tears won't stop.

A very special nurse from Bob's team, Jeani, comes in to see me, and just in time. She is helping me keep my eye on the prize. She sits with me to encourage me while Jason is at work. She tells me, holding my hand as I cry, that we will take the next hour together and get through it somehow. And if that is too much to think about, we will take five minutes. Or one minute. Even one breath at a time, if we have to.

CHAPTER 29

THE POTTY TRAINING

When I decided it was time to start potty training, the kids were two weeks shy of their second birthday. I was tired of changing diapers. I was so over paying for diapers. I wanted to be free. So I made a plan. We got up one day at the crack of dawn. Actually, it hadn't even cracked yet. It was pitch black outside. It was so blasted early because I wanted to make sure everyone's pants were still dry. I knew each and every one of them possessed the ability to stay dry all night. They'd each done it, just not consistently or all four at the same time. After a long night, they'd hang out during those early morning hours playing in their rooms when I was too tired to drag my exhausted body out of bed and tend to them right away. Often that morning play would transition into the Sesame Street hour when I'd release them to watch their show, and I'd crawl back under the warm covers for just a *few more minutes*. During the delayed attention, their status from dry-all-night converted to oops-I-need-a-diaper-change. So to avoid any accidents, about three hours before Big Bird even woke up that fateful morning, I dragged four sleep-confused toddlers from their miniature beds, marched them into the kitchen, told them to down about three gallons each of apple juice, then led them into the bathroom. We had four potty chairs. We had books. We had sippy cups. We had a jar filled to the brim with M&Ms. We were set.

The four potty chairs included three "stand alone" units lined up in front of the bathtub and one insert that went over the regular toilet seat. They took turns sitting on the Big Potty. A husband of an older friend asked me one day how the potty training was going. He also commented about how amazed he was that we re-plumbed the bathroom to have four little toilets in it. He simply couldn't imagine doing that. (I couldn't help but think he wasn't very involved in his own children's potty training.) He clearly had no idea that you bought little plastic toilets and manually emptied them. No extra plumbing involved.

That very first time we tried, Molly was successful. With enthusiastic praise, I counted out and awarded her two M&Ms, telling the boys that they too could have some candy if only they'd tinkle in the potty. (If they pooped, they'd get three.) Besides the blatant bribery, while we waited I read stories, we sang songs, we discussed Bert and Ernie and Cookie Monster. Because of the immediate results with Molly, I thought for sure it wouldn't be long before they all graduated to Big Kid Pants.

But the process took longer than I had hoped. Hour after hour, day after day, we sat on those potties, working to use them instead of the Pull-Ups. We even tried without Pull-Ups so they'd have to deal with having wet, drippy cloth underpants. Still, no luck. One day, the kids were seated for their mandatory pit stop in the middle of their play. The phone rang. I had to leave the bathroom for a second. Really. It was only a second. When I came back in, each contender wore a darling smile and bubbled with giggles. And they were each on different potties from when I'd left, and one of the potties had tinkle in it. But I had no idea who'd done it. And they weren't telling. They were hardly speaking in coherent language at that point in their young lives anyway. They sure weren't going to waste words on outing whoever had made the deposit. My dilemma was, do I give everyone M&Ms or no one? I decided everyone should taste them. (Including me.) They probably planned the whole thing to get M&Ms on the sly. But why not reward them anyway? They came off pretty clever by my book. And tasting chocolate for the first time might entice them to find their elimination on-off switch to earn more candies.

Molly was soon competent in the fine art of using the potty, even mastering the technique of putting her poo in there too. (She also was too good at unwinding the entire roll of toilet paper onto the floor.) She could even exhibit initiative and take herself, if she only needed to tinkle. Spencer was her biggest cheerleader. Whenever she used the potty, he pointed into it then clapped exuberantly, saying with a great, big grin, "Maw paw mmm," which translated meant, "Molly potty, M&M." Because of Molly's success and growing independence, I put a potty in her bedroom so that when she woke in the morning before I got up and processed children out of their rooms by taking down their doorway gates, she could use her little chair and keep her pants dry. The only problem, her roommate Spencer loved "helping" and knew a crucial step of the process was emptying the bowl under the seat after use. He couldn't leave well enough alone, and as soon as Molly filled the bowl, he pulled it out and dumped it on the carpet next to the door. No matter *how many millions of times* I told him *not* to do that, every single morning he beat me to it and poured it out. Washing the carpet every day was getting much more tiresome than changing a diaper. I was beginning to think it wasn't worth it.

I had a friend with a three-year-old son, twin toddler girls, and a baby. Once the baby came, she gave up on potty training and told her twins, "I'm just going to let your husbands potty train you. I can't *do* this!" I knew then not to sweat it. Certainly by high school, worst case, mine would have it worked out. They wouldn't need to wait until they were married, surely. Why beat myself up about it?

But the trouble was, I really—I mean *really*—wanted to get away from diapers. The cost was killing us, plus the constant chore of changing them was becoming unbearable. Changing poopy pants from a three-year-old is *much* more taxing than from a three-pound premie. And doing it four times in a row, over and over? I was so over it.

Even today, I have a crisp, clear memory of the day that we used our last diaper. It took nine months after that early dark winter morning, but we finally got there. It took till summer and warm weather, which came with lighter, easy-to-shed clothing, for them to master the skills, when a wiggling boy who'd waited almost too long to dash to the potty could finally and independently do what he needed to do in time to keep his pants dry. It was definitely time to end the madness and get everyone into their Toy Story underwear.

CHAPTER 30

NOTES ON BEING THIRTY-TWO WEEKS

Dang it, I'm back on magnesium sulfate, though it's not nearly as wicked as the last time because they gave me a *way* smaller dose. Each time we have one of these redos, they're doing a little better to manage the doses with all of my med sensitivities. But even though I'm not suffering to the degree I was before, this certainly can't be called a walk in the park. And as far as walking, by the way, I can't do that again. This stupid medicine—which I guess I shouldn't call stupid since it is getting me through a few more hours of pregnancy—means I have to have a catheter again and I can't get out of bed anymore.

It's Wednesday night and the hospital corridors have quieted again and the sky through my window is black. Tomorrow I am thirty-two weeks. Can you believe it? That's seven months pregnant. We've been doing this for *seven months*. For the last measurement they took of my belly, I was bigger than a ten-and-a-half-month pregnant woman, if there is such a thing. That was a while ago. They don't even get out the tape measure anymore. What's the point? Sure, the Pink Ladies are probably hovering outside my door wanting to find out my exact girth to see who of them won their betting pool, but they'll be out of luck. My nurses have decided to just say I'm big. Really big.

Jason hands me the camera and stands next to the wall where he just pinned up the Christmas cards that I've scissored into the number "32." He always hangs the numbers up at night before he leaves so I can see them first thing in the morning and look at them all day long and be inspired while he is at work. (Yes, by the way, he got his job back the second week of January.) From my floating air bed I prop the camera on my giant baby bump—or baby *mountain* at this point—and aim the lens at Jason who is doing a Vanna White for the "32" on the bulletin board. I snap a picture. It's a terrific milestone, this.

Tomorrow morning my obstetrician is leaving town for five days for some ridiculous thing he's committed himself to without asking me first. I can't believe the timing. It's terrible. Completely unacceptable. What am *I* supposed to do? He is scheduled to be on call through the night. Then at seven when the sun dawns, he'll be gone. He is the only doctor in town who has delivered quadruplets before, and I want him to deliver mine. As reticent as he is, I've grown quite fond of and dependent on him. I don't know how I am going to wait five more hours, let alone five more days. But I guess I'll have to. I don't want some fill-in doctor waltzing in and doing something dangerous from lack of experience and put any of us at greater risk. There is so much for the obstetrician to think about as he is cutting me wide open. Dr. Loquacious explained to me a little about the considerations and concerns, like my risk of exsanguinating, and how he must stay on top of everything to prevent that. When he makes the first incision, he will have to cut through a lot of placenta to get to any babies. Those are minefields of major arteries. He will need to work fast and furious to get everyone out before any of us bleeds to death. And that's just the one example he's told me about. I desperately want him to be there. *Need* him to be there. He hasn't offered to cancel his trip, so I'm going to have to buckle up and find some kind of new reserve to wait for him to get his fancy leather loafers and bare ankles back into town.

After Jason puts the camera away, he tucks me in like he does each night, surrounding my blimp of a body with nearly a dozen pillows to support the sore parts and keep the boney parts from hurting each other. I love the ritual. It is a major relief to get repositioned on a new side and have freshly fluffed soft cushions around me. He turns on quiet music and dims the lights to a nightlight level. We kiss goodnight, and he leaves for home. I'll see him tomorrow afternoon when he gets off work and comes to the hospital.

Cozily snuggled in my sea of pillows, I settle in for the night. I close my eyes and let my mind empty. In spite of my underlying discomfort, as a cassette tape of Enya quietly serenades me from my boom box sitting on the shelf, I fall asleep.

And I wake up again. It seems like Jason just left. By the red glow of the bedside clock, it's a little past 2:00 a.m. It's quiet and dark. And I realize I've awakened because I've *wet the bed*. I haven't wet the bed for decades. But the way things happen now, who knows how my body will betray me? There's one thing though—I have a catheter in. I shouldn't be able to wet the bed. I turn on my call light and Hanna, my night nurse, comes in.

"It feels like I wet the bed."

"Hmm. Maybe your catheter is leaking."

She checks to see if the tube is kinked or has some other problem, which she can't find. She calls another nurse to help her change the bed with me in it and place a clean Chux pad on the sheets beneath me. They both say several times they're confident it's just urine. This makes me disappointed because a couple of days ago something leaked and I had to have a horribly painful exam to see if I was dilating. But now as I lie here, paying attention to what is happening, I'm kind of thinking this might actually be amniotic fluid because each time I contract, it leaks.

To be certain, Hanna does a "fern test," a test with a microscope slide that will show the fluid spreading out like a fern if it is in fact amniotic fluid. She is out of the room for a little bit. Then she returns.

And the test is *positive*. This is such good news.

It's only about four hours before my doctor will turn off his pager and go off duty, but for now, he is still on call. Hanna pages him, and after a short wait, he arrives in my room, his brown eyes a little sleepy, his hair a mess.

"How do you feel?" Dr. Loquacious asks.

"I gush fluid every time I have a contraction."

"You're going to have the babies today," he says matter-of-factly.

"I am so happy," I say breathlessly.

He says to Hanna, "I'm going to do an ultrasound to see the position of the babies."

She gets the machine and Dr. Loquacious spends a long time quietly and intently studying where each of my babies is.

When he finishes, he says to Hanna, "Turn off the mag at 5:30." Then to me, "We'll try to wait until morning to deliver, but if you start labor with the mag off, we'll have to go sooner."

Wow. Deliver today. I'm so relieved. For so many reasons. My mind can't wrap around it completely yet, but I know this is good.

He leaves, I think to go nap before the big show. How cool is this? He's going to delay his departure and stay on duty to do the delivery. And I didn't even have to threaten or bribe him or anything. One of my kids must have been listening when he told us he was leaving town and decided to help me out here. Someone kicked in the right spot and busted through his bag. The timing couldn't have been better. When we find out who did it, he or she is going to be my favorite. For a year, at least.

"Should I call Jason?" I ask Hanna.

She thinks I should. I call him and he happens to be up having a bowl of Cheerios because he can't sleep. I tell him it's time, someone's bag of water broke, and the delivery is going to happen at sunrise.

Hanna tells me I've been put on the OR schedule for 7:00 a.m., the delivery to take place during the change of shift when twice as many people will be working during the overlap between day and night staff.

Jason arrives by 4:30 a.m. and we spend our last hours of being just a couple waiting, simply sitting, quietly talking together in my room. There is no way I can get back to sleep.

After Hanna turns off the mag sulfate and it begins to clear from my body, the contractions start to increase pretty quickly, but not so much that we have to do anything about it except maybe breathe a little more intentionally through them. It's not too uncomfortable. Nothing like six weeks ago when my head was going to explode with each contraction.

At 6:00 a.m. Hanna suggests to Jason that he clear my room of my personal belongings and take them to the car before everything gets crazy, because after the delivery I will be going to a different room on the postpartum floor. With Hanna's help, he gathers up my things, then carts the nearly two months' worth of accumulated possessions to the car. When he finishes and returns to my room, he tells me about a couple different groups of excited hospital personnel he encountered in the corridor and elevator. He overheard them sharing among themselves the morning's breaking gossip that "the quads are about to be delivered!" He said he didn't tell them he was the daddy-to-be of said quads, and he just listened with a private little smile, marveling at how quickly news travels, and that other people are so interested in our business.

Jason went to call Jeani, who has become a special companion on the journey, to make sure she knows to come to the delivery. We're told she has already arrived at the hospital so we assume she's on her way to us.

Hanna gives Jason a pack of disposable blue OR wear to put on.

Moments before the clock strikes seven, my nurses help me transfer my unwieldy body from my air bed onto a gurney—not an easy maneuver in my condition. With Jason walking at my side, they roll me down the hall, through the labor and delivery department, and into the surgical area. My doctor and his plus-one are there by the scrub sinks drinking coffee. I say hello, but they don't return my greeting. They are both very sober.

We roll into a crowded operating room whirring with

noise and energetic excitement as multiple groups of caregivers chatter and laugh while they prepare their work areas. Each baby will get a team of specialists, which includes a NICU nurse or two, a respiratory therapist, a nurse practitioner, plus a neonatologist and pediatrician to help oversee the whole process. And for me there is my obstetrician, his plus-one—another obstetrician to assist him with the surgery—a scrub tech, a circulating nurse, my anesthesiologist Dr. Johnson, and probably a few more nurses thrown in for good measure.

As soon as Dr. Loquacious enters, he sternly tells everyone to hush, silencing the room like a strict teacher would shush a third grade class entering a museum for a fieldtrip.

When I see him, I ask with a lighthearted smile, "Have you got your bags packed yet for your trip?"

Again, he doesn't answer, apparently distracted with thinking about how this whole thing is going to go down. Did I mention he's a pretty serious fellow?

Several people help me scoot onto the narrow surgical table. For a few minutes I have to curl up on my side so the anesthesiologist can give me a spinal in my lower back. He tells me to pull my knees up to my chest.

Yeah right. Did he not *look* at me?

He says to do the best I can.

So I pull my knees up probably about a centimeter more, and a nurse tries to help me go a bit farther. Dr. Johnson swabs my back with a cold wet wash, then administers the spinal. He does a great job. He's fast, and I hardly felt anything.

They roll me onto my back.

"Will you put my knees down? My knees are up. I can't move them."

"No, they're down."

"Are you sure? I feel them bent up."

"That's because your brain is remembering your last feeling before I numbed you," Dr. Johnson explains. "Your legs are flat."

"Really? Because it really doesn't feel like it." I can't look to see; they're so quick that they've already covered me up with drapes and cut off my view.

I look at Jason. "Are you sure they're not bent up?"

His eyes are looking at me through his glasses over the surgical mask covering the lower half of his face. A tissue-thin blue bouffant hat covers his head. His muffled voice assures me from behind the mask that my legs are stretched out flat. He's tucked in up by my left shoulder, sitting next to Dr. Johnson. My arm is strapped down on an arm board straight out to the side of the OR table like a crucifixion.

The surgeons have clipped up a cloth drape like a little curtain at my collarbones, so I can't see anything below my chin. While they prep my belly beyond the drape, I talk about nothing too consequential with Jason and Dr. Johnson. We're excited but calm. And we're careful to keep our voices down because our head doctor shushed everyone, and I guess that means us too. Besides, I don't want to distract him. I want him to do well, to think clearly, to keep us all alive. Jason can see beyond the drape that's blocking my view. He doesn't seem stressed by any of what's going on around us, just taking it in. My "nurse mode" has rubbed off on him, I think. I've told him so many hospital stories over the years, including gross inappropriate things at the dinner table, he is unfazed about the bloody aspect of what he is about to experience.

I'm saying something to Dr. Johnson when someone shouts, *It's a boy!* and a little voice squeaks.

Whoa. I didn't even know they'd started. Apparently,

I'm having babies *right now*! That quiet doctor of mine. He'd used a silent hand sign for the scalpel. I must pay attention.

Jason is standing now. He says, "He has a lot of hair."

Within seconds, another shout from one of the nurses—*It's another boy!* Then *It's a girl!* Babies A, B, and C are born at 7:47 a.m. When the clock clicks over to 7:48, I hear, *It's another boy!*, and Baby D has arrived.

Little voices squeak around the room while Jason and I await some word of how they are faring. Jason can see a little of what is going on, and he tells me about it, though it isn't much because of all the people gathered around each warming bed. The fact that I can hear their voices is a good sign to me, knowing they are breathing, not yet intubated, and making a bit of a fuss, even if small fusses.

In no time, the first team rolls a warming bed toward the door past Jason and me to take the first baby to the NICU. The bed stops for a moment, parked as close to my face as possible. I see Molly for the first time. They pull off her pink and blue striped knit cap so we can see her better. She has a lot of hair too. She's a cute baby. And she's pink, wiggling, doing the things she should.

Moments after they're gone, the next team and bed roll past with another baby—Charlie this time. I know they need to get a move on to the NICU to do a thorough assessment and give any supportive care required. I know the drill so well, I am relaxed and confident, certain that the teams will take good care of our kids.

Then suddenly, a feeling changes inside of me.

"Did you just give me something? I feel like…you're putting me under…."

Dr. Johnson says, "You're losing a lot of blood. You're blood pressure is dropping—there, I gave you something that should make you feel better."

It works fast. But then almost as quickly, the awful

feeling comes rushing back.

"I'm going to throw up," I choke out, panting, losing my breath, feeling like the bottom is falling out of my existence. My blood pressure is plummeting again. I feel so sick, so weak, if I weren't already lying down, I'd be on the ground. I am bleeding out.

Jason sees blood everywhere, even running down the sides of the table and filling the shoe of the assistant surgeon, who curses, slips his foot out of his clog, and shakes out his leg, splattering blood across the tile floor. All the while, he's lending his hand to Dr. Loquacious, who is scrambling to stop the hemorrhaging as fast as he can.

Dr. Johnson helps me turn my head toward the emesis basin he is holding by the side of my face. He says matter-of-factly, "This is why we don't let patients eat before surgery." I retch nothing into the kidney-shaped basin, and there's no feeling or motion past my shoulders. I heave, but all movement stops above my collarbones, and it feels like I don't have a body anymore. My sight narrows and black spots converge in my vision.

This time I black out enough that I lose track of time and what's going on in the room. By the time I stabilize, gain consciousness and become alert, and can perceive what is happening in the room again, the other two babies have already been transported out of the OR.

It takes a while for the surgeons to do what is needed to stabilize me, clean me out, and stitch me closed again. I can feel pressure and tugging deep inside as they manipulate my organs in ways I don't want to know or think about. I have to will myself not to worry about it too much. But it feels pretty awful, and I wish I didn't have to experience this part.

When they finish, Dr. Loquacious wishes me well, says

everything is satisfactory, and he'll see me in a few days. His assisting surgeon, his plus-one with the shoe full of blood, will take care of me while he's gone. Then he leaves, I can only assume, to pack his suitcase and get to the airport before he misses his flight.

CHAPTER 31

THE TRAIN TRIP

Nearly every summer since the kids were two we've gone to Minnesota to see Jason's family around the Fourth of July, meeting up with his brother and his family and Jason's sister and her family, staying at the big house on the farm with Jack and Jason's stepmom. The first time, we decided to take the train, which provided several advantages: neither of us had to drive the sixteen hour trip, it was by far less expensive than flying (with half-price tickets for children, which was great because ours were only half-sized people), and we could travel at night when the kids would be sleeping. We'd board, settle in, and sleep our way to vacation. What more could one want? The only drawback, and it was kind of significant, was that the train, the California Zephyr, didn't go where we needed it to.

CZ's route took it from Denver to Chicago, but the tracks along the way ran through southern Iowa. We needed to get to Minnesota, the state way up on the north side of Iowa. To get to Minnesota by train, we'd have to travel all the way to Chicago then board a different train and backtrack northwest to get to St. Paul (more than 100 miles north of the farm), adding another day's travel plus more money spent on tickets and more time corralling four two-year-olds on a train. So we arranged with Jack—who loved to take road trips—to drive down to a small town called Osceola, Iowa (four hours south of the farm), and pick us up at a dinky train depot there.

With transportation figured out, everything else started falling into place. I got the brainy idea to sew us new clothes for the trip. I found some clearance light cotton madras plaid that would be terrific in the Minnesota summer heat, and it came in all the kids' colors, so I made them coordinated outfits. Then I went nuts and made myself a jumper out of the same fabric in a fifth color. Then I went completely off the deep end and made Jason a matching tailored shirt in the sixth color. He was very kind and didn't balk (he should have balked), and he agreed to wear it.

Our dear friend Linda kindly offered to drive us to Denver on the evening of our departure. The train would leave the station at 9:00 p.m., travel all night, then drop us off in Iowa at 8:00 a.m. We loaded into her van, and she delivered us to Union Station in downtown Denver without incident in plenty of time. The kids were excited, and so were we. It was going to be a great adventure.

After checking in, we learned our train was going to be delayed for a short time. So we settled in on the old wooden benches to wait, hoping the extra hour would pass quickly without any meltdowns. It was already well past bedtime, and we needed the kids to hold on a little longer. As updates came in, the announcer kept pushing out the arrival time of the train that would pick us up and take us on toward Chicago. Finally, they admitted a train had derailed in front of ours, and they didn't know how long it would be. They told us it could be several hours, and we should go home and wait on stand-by. Since the drive home would be ninety minutes one way, and we wouldn't ask Linda to drive us back a second time, I called and woke up my eighty-four year old grandpa who lived in a tiny house less than three miles from the train station and asked if we could sleep at his place for a few hours. Linda delivered us there, and we quickly got the kids to sleep on a blanket in the middle of the living room floor. Every hour or so I called the station for an update, and finally at 5:00 a.m., they said we should return to the station. I called and ordered a Yellow Cab, explaining we needed them to send a van so we would have enough seatbelts for all six of us, including four child car seats. But when the cab drove up beneath the street light in front of Grandpa's curb, it was only a small sedan. When we protested and said it didn't have enough seats or seatbelts, the cabbie assured us we wouldn't need them. A taxi is like a city bus, he said like it was good news, and no seatbelts are required. Like being exempt from the law meant we'd be exempt from danger. With trepidation, we let him stow the car seats in his trunk, and Jason and I piled into the back seat of the cab, each of us holding two sleepy kids. It felt like tempting fate to not use car seats, but we didn't know what else to do. We could only hold tight and pray we'd get through Denver without any mishaps.

Once safely at the train station, we found an empty bench—heavy, high-backed wooden pew-like seating from the original train depot—and we sat down and prepared to wait. By now, the kids were disrupted enough that they weren't going back to sleep. They were dazed, sitting and staring in silence. It so happened that in front of where the six of us sat on the bench was one of those velvet ropes swung between two brass posts used to direct people in line. Before long, a crowd was growing on the other side of the plush barrier. The cluster of people were talking among themselves while watching us, some even pointing at us who were all six dressed in matching madras plaid, announcing to the world that we were some kind of spectacle. It was impossible to miss four little kids the exact same size lined up in identical clothes of various hues. One of the observers finally worked up the nerve to ask us directly about the kids, instead of talking about us like we couldn't hear them. Once we started interacting, a flood of questions and comments came. It was like we were on exhibition at the state fair. For a long while after we answered their questions they simply watched us. But we had to be about the business of parenting and managing four tired, hungry, and disrupted toddlers. Spencer became especially mischievous, provoking his siblings. Several times I had to tell him, "Okay, ornery, leave Pierce alone," or "Ornery, be nice!" By the time the train finally came, it was ten hours late, arriving at 7:00 a.m., one hour before we were supposed to have been dropped off in Iowa. We had one diaper left per kid, one juice box each, and only a few gold fish. It was going to be a long day.

Once we moved our pile of belongings onto the train, including four car seats, six people's luggage for a week, and all our activity bags and what was left of our survival supplies, we found seats and settled in. Running on about two hours of piecemeal sleep wasn't going to help me cope at all. What a relief when we started rolling down the tracks. We'd adjusted the plans with Jack by phone, telling him that we were already nearly out of supplies.

Before long, we noticed there was a lot of activity in our train car, with many people squeezing past our two rows of seats, slowing to stare and whisper. Finally, a woman stopped who had been the one asking us the most questions behind the rope back at the station. She turned around in the aisle to face the group following her, with us centered between them, and she explained who we were, that the kids were quadruplets, and how old they were. She said she didn't know all their names yet. But she knew the one in blue was (she used a nasal French accent) Henry, or *Aun-REE*, as it would sound to us. Turns out, she'd formed tour groups and brought people by in shifts to see us, relaying the information she'd ascertained while we were on display behind the rope. She'd heard me call Spencer "ornery" several times and interpreted that to be his French name. I don't know if she charged for her tours, but I should have insisted on a cut of the take.

We were so exhausted. When 1:00 p.m. came around, we were relieved the activity around the kids died away, and we got them settled down for naps. By the time we landed in Iowa and got off the train, we were out of everything (including vim and vigor) and could only hope that Jack knew how to buy diapers. It was with great relief that not only did he bring a large box of the correct size, but also a Suburban with seatbelts for each of us, and sandwiches and juice boxes for everyone. Once we ate and the kids' diapers were changed, we had only to face four more hours in the car—which got us to the farm long after midnight. By then, we were more than ready to start our vacay.

If I'd known how hard it would be to spend a week in Minnesota, with distant relatives arranging secret meeting times to show up and gawk at us (we should have kept the velvet rope), or trying to take care of four toddlers in someone else's home, which not only wasn't baby-proofed but was still basically a construction zone with exposed electric outlets and three stories of unfinished, roughed-in staircases without railings and balconies without banisters, I would have turned around and gone home that first moment the train official suggested it. For the train ride back to Denver, I dressed every person in a completely different outfit and made eye contact with exactly no one. And when we got home, I gave Jason's shirt to my dad. Jason wouldn't be needing it. Ever. So much for matching outfits. Never again would I make *that* mistake.

CHAPTER 32

NOTES ON BEING PARENTS

Jason is in the NICU seeing how each of our children is doing and meeting them more personally than what we got with the quick drive-by staged in the OR. My anesthesiologist, Dr. Johnson, and my nurse brought me here to the recovery room, where I need to stay for the next hour or so to make sure I'm stable and doing well enough to move to the postpartum floor.

As I'm lying here, I cannot express how *fabulous* it is to lie flat on my back. And without passing out. To have all those little people taken out of me, plus the wonder of a numbing spinal, has left me more comfortable than I remember being possible.

I place my hands on my deflated abdomen, over my womb who has become like the best girlfriend I would ever want. Now she's like a punctured rubber ball that's lost all the air and is left droopy, empty. She's had all the stuffing knocked out of her, literally. *We did it.* She's done well, and I tell her in my thoughts, like she's a whole person, an entity of her own. She's like the companion who has gone to battle with me, who went through hell and back alongside of me no matter what we faced. She kept going, never giving up, fighting till the end as long as we needed her. I smile, spending a moment in gratefulness, as I realize where we are, how far we've come, and what we've accomplished.

Jeani comes in, having just heard, and is disappointed to have missed *everything.* She never got the message or knew I was delivering. I feel so disappointed for her too. She has done so much to help me get this far. But even though disappointed, she jumps right in to do what she can now to help. As a trained obstetrical nurse, she checks my fundus to make sure my uterus is firm and contracted like it should be, which would keep me from losing even more blood. She finds that it's as soft as mush and I'm bleeding way too much. Jeani pushes her fist down deeply into my deflated belly and massages hard toward my spine. Thank goodness for a good spinal! She gets a contraction started, which will clamp down on the blood vessels and stop the bleeding. My recovery nurse jumps in to help, and the two of them clean me up and get me settled comfortably again. Jeani goes to the NICU to find Jason and to meet our new babies who she helped to keep safe.

I look up and standing in the doorway is Lisa, my best friend from nursing school, holding a handful of brilliant yellow daffodils.

She smiles brightly. "I just came to visit. I went to your room but they sent me over here. I didn't know you'd delivered," she says a little embarrassed.

It doesn't matter that she's crashed my delivery. I am excited to share the moment with my good friend. I wave her into the room the rest of the way, and we visit while my nurse continues to work around us, checking my incision and vital signs. Jason comes in too and gives us a report about how everyone is doing, which is still good, all things considered.

After Lisa goes, it's time for me to leave the recovery room. On the way to my new room on the postpartum floor, my nurse wheels my gurney into the NICU first so I can meet my babies. Jason and I are together now, and we go to spend time at each baby's bedside. A nurse carries around a Polaroid to snap photos of us as we make our rounds. They've put all four of the kids in the same section of the NICU, an area that only holds four beds, so our quadruplets are in the same room, close together and easy to see at once. They're about five feet apart—each in his or her own corner—two along one wall and the other two across the tile from them along the other wall.

Each bed has a sign posted above it with the letters A through D, going clockwise around the room. Baby A is immediately on our left when we enter, and they push my gurney alongside his warming bed. He's lying on the flat, open mattress that is right at the level of my stretcher. This is Spencer, our firstborn. His tiny body is nestled between white and blue cotton receiving blankets rolled to cradle him and help him feel loved and safe. He's wearing a striped knit stocking hat, tiny blue booties, and an itty bitty diaper. I reach over and touch him for the first time, stroking his cheek, his arm, a leg. His skin is soft and warm. He's crying, looking sad that he had to come out so soon.

But I send him thoughts to be happy because he's my favorite today. It was he who broke his amniotic bag. He was the one listening when my doctor said he was leaving town. He's my hero who rescued me on this day when I didn't know how I could go on any longer.

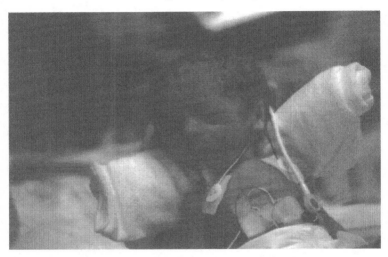

Spencer weighs two pounds, eleven ounces—the runt of my litter. He is also the least stable, needing the highest oxygen and most medical support. Thankfully he doesn't need to be on a ventilator, just an apparatus called CPAP (Continuous Positive Airway Pressure), which pushes air via his nose into his lungs to keep the millions of teeny air sacs open. The best news is he is taking all of his breaths himself. There are lines into his umbilicus, wires running to his EKG electrodes and pulse ox, a peripheral IV in his left arm, and a few other connections to monitor him, but I don't really see any of those things. I've spent years working with all of this equipment myself with past patients, so it doesn't phase me in the least. I look past it and only see my new precious baby. Jason seems completely relaxed too. We couldn't have been better prepared for this chapter of our lives. My past experiences had to have given me a less stressful pregnancy, to have helped me get this far, to have given them each the best environment to incubate and best possible chance to live.

After meeting Spencer, we roll over to meet Baby B—Pierce—who's second in the birth order, weighing in at a whopping three pounds, twelve ounces—more than a pound heavier than Spencer.

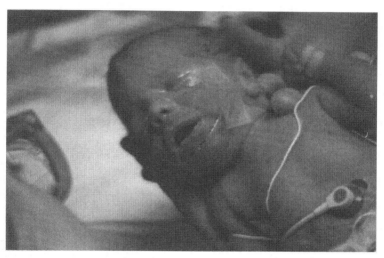

With the head of my stretcher raised to help hold me up, I prop myself sideways on my elbow, and Pierce's nurse, Sharon, lifts him a couple inches off the warming bed mattress, working within the slack of all the tubes and wires to place him into my outstretched hands. I hold him hovering over his mattress as I lean from my gurney. Jason is right behind me, his hand resting on my shoulder, leaning in with me to look Pierce right in the face for the first time. Though the biggest, he is the next medically critical after Spencer. Size doesn't determine strength or health. He needs nearly as much oxygen and CPAP as Spencer. At least he is sleeping, looking content and comfortable, nestled in my hands. Even though he is asleep, he is my favorite.

After a few minutes, he needs his CPAP and oxygen back on. Sharon takes him and lowers him onto his mattress again, nestling him among the soft rolls of blankets, and we move on to meet the baby in the next bed.

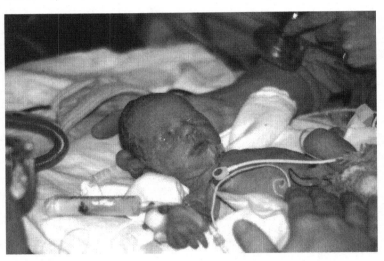

Baby C—Molly. She is doing terrifically. Three pounds, three ounces. They're already lowering her oxygen levels. It's typical. Statistically, premie girls do better than premie boys. She is a tough little cookie, and she is my favorite. All of her vitals are stable. She's wearing pink crocheted booties with pompons on the ties. Even with a little tube down her throat to keep her stomach drained, she is tolerating it well and resting without any apparent distress. We couldn't ask for her to be doing any better, considering the circumstances.

Lastly, we move over, and Jason introduces me to Charles. We're already calling him by the nickname Charlie. He's my favorite. His birth weight is two pounds, fifteen ounces. Sweet little thing. He has a swollen black eye where it has been pressed against a flattened spot on the side of Pierce's head. There just wasn't enough room inside of me for all four of them not to be smashed. They've put some ointment on his inflamed eye, and it's gooey, glistening, and puffy. Poor baby. In spite of the shiner his brother gave him, he's holding steady and not far behind Molly in his progress, requiring less oxygen support almost as quickly as his sister.

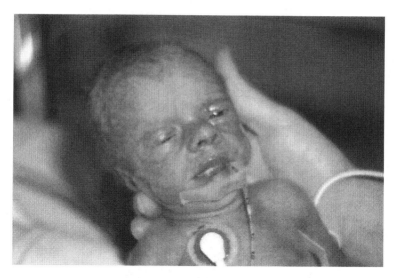

After spending as much time as we can with each of our babies, it is time for me to go to the postpartum floor and check into my new digs and let my nurses make sure I'm still recovering well. I'm wondering if I might be able to get food soon. Oh, to eat again. The relief of being empty is extraordinary.

My postpartum nurse, with the help of my recovery room nurse, gets me settled into my unfamiliar room and bed. Though I'd rather stay in the NICU with my babies, I need to rest. Having an incision the size of the Mississippi River means that as my spinal wears off and my sensation comes back, I'm going to need to stay close to my room so my nurse can give me pain shots.

Every time I try to sit up, my head swims. I couldn't get up and go anywhere if my life depended on it. With all the blood loss, plus the fact my heart has apparently forgotten how to pump uphill after eighteen weeks on bed rest, the oxygen isn't getting to my brain fast enough.

They roll into my room an incredibly powerful breast pump with instructions for me to use it every two hours. I'm going to try this breastfeeding thing as long as possible. I want to nurse my babies. Maybe I'm crazy, but it's tremendously important to me.

Jason keeps me updated on everybody's status, visiting them while I can't leave my bed. I make a few phone calls, starting with Cyndi, to let our families know the babies are here. By afternoon, those who live in town start coming to the hospital. While I rest, Jason escorts them to the NICU and introduces them to our kids. Cyndi brings two boxes of chocolate cigars for Jason, one pink box with the candy cigars wrapped in pink foil, and one blue box full of metallic blue chocolate stogies. She has a mild cold, left from getting wiped out after donating blood, so she wears a mask but still goes in with Jason to get a look at the babies from a safe distance.

While they're off getting acquainted, I pull up my rolling bedside table with the menu order sheet and golf pencil, and I study the delightful food options to plan out my meals, now that I can eat again. We are going to party tonight.

CHAPTER 33

THE SNOWMAN IN THE KITCHEN

One day when my children were two, we were having a terrible day. I was cranky; they were cranky. I was feeling trapped and alone, overwhelmed, depressed. It was snowing, and the barometer was dropping. And so was my disposition. I had had about all I could deal with. My patience was pushed near the point I would stop being able to cope. So I called our good friend Linda who'd helped with the kids from the beginning. I'd never asked someone to come bail me out before. This was different from inviting over the Quad Squad who helped feed babies and wash bottles. I was desperate. I needed someone to come give me a break. I told Linda things felt really bad and asked if she could come and rescue me. She had a prior commitment and couldn't come, but she said she would pray for me. I hung up the phone thinking, *Great. That was my only idea. Now what am I going to do?* I went upstairs for a personal timeout and stared out the kitchen window at the falling snow. I debated my options. If I sent them outside in the snow, I would have to bundle each of them up—four snow suits, four hats, four coats, eight boots, eight mittens. Then they would go outside and get sopping wet and cold. They'd come back inside with four runny noses, eighty cold fingers and toes, all the layers soggy and stuck to their skin, nearly impossible to tug off. I didn't think I had the courage to face that monumental task this particular morning.

I turned, and they were spilling into the kitchen from the stairwell, as they never could let me out of their sight for more than a few minutes. In sheer desperation, I began to pull out the snow gear. I was going to have to buck up and face the overwhelming task of suiting them up and deal with the work. We were all too antsy and cranky to only stand there and cry at each other.

Then an idea came from heaven. It seemed that Linda's prayers were being heard.

I shoved the kitchen table and chairs over against the far wall and told the kids, "Wait here a minute."

I tugged on my own boots and ran out the back door. I returned carrying a bucket of snow and dumped it in the middle of the kitchen on the tile floor. The kids stared at me with wide eyes and disbelief. They knew for sure Mom had gone off the deep end.

I hauled in several more buckets of snow when finally Spencer, the "water baby" of the four—the boy who absolutely *loved* water any time, any place, any form—shook off the shock of seeing me do something so absurdly wonderful and toddled over toward the growing pile to touch the cold snow. Once he broke the ice, the rest jumped in. Soon I was in the middle of it with them, laughing and throwing snow balls around the kitchen.

We built a little snowman, pulling forks from the silverware drawer and sticking them into the sides of the snowman for his arms. We found a carrot in the refrigerator for his nose, and some other loose vegetables to make his eyes. We completed his style with Spencer's eyeglasses to give him an academic look. Once he started to melt, a thin film of water under his frozen body made him as slick as a hockey puck, and we took turns pushing him to each other around the kitchen, seeing how far he could go. Eventually, when the snow was turning to mush, I used the dustpan to scoop the chunks into the sink and a mop to soak up the leftover water.

What a gift the day turned out to be. We laughed and played together, truly enjoying some of the fast-fleeting days of childhood, and I even got my kitchen floor cleaned in the process. Linda's prayers brought about so much more than if she'd just come over and watched the kids while I went and hid in the bathroom.

CHAPTER 34

NOTES ON BEING RESOLUTE

Later in the afternoon on the day our children are born, my parents come to visit and bring their video camera. Jason takes them on a tour of the NICU, and they record videotapes of each of the babies, sometimes filming the floor or their shoes while the off-screen conversation continues because they don't really know how to use their new camera. But they do get some good shots that I'm sure we'll cherish for years to come. We don't have our own video recorder so I'm glad they're getting some home movies for us.

By late evening everyone has left, and Jason and I are completely worn out. What a day! Considering we've been awake since 2:00 a.m., it's amazing we don't fall asleep the second we hold still. But we're too wired to do that. Instead of sleeping, we watch a horror movie on the hospital cable channel, snuggling next to each other in my bed. It's the only movie on and frankly quite gross, but even a creepy movie can't truly get under my skin. The contentment I feel is thick and lovely. All is well, and everyone is doing great for being born two months early. Everything worked out so that I got my own doctor for the delivery. With the spinal still numbing my incision the size of the Mississippi, I'm not too uncomfortable. I can eat and breathe again, lie on my back, and I've finally met my babies face to face. I couldn't be happier.

Through the night I'm awake often to use the breast pump, to reposition, get meds, or drink water to replace my lost fluids.

In the morning, I have to start trying to dangle my feet toward the floor from the edge of my bed. But I am having the hardest time staying conscious whenever I raise my head high. I wish they'd give me the blood Cyndi donated for me. (For all the trouble she went through, if they're not going to give it to me, they ought to give it back to her.) It would make all the difference for me. But for some reason they don't want to if it's not completely necessary. Personally, I'd call this completely necessary. But I'm not the one making the decisions.

Besides my little problem with staying conscious, by this second post-op day, being cleaved in two has put a painful damper on my mobility. I mean, have you *seen* the Mississippi? That's one humongous river. Man, this hurts, now that the spinal has worn completely off. My incision starts below my belly button and goes down almost to the Gulf of Mexico. But I am determined to get up and get to my babies. The postpartum nurses must be overly busy because I rarely see them. It seems like I'm the one doing most of my own nursing care. At least I'm an experienced postpartum nurse—though never for a mom of higher multiples. But I've got this. I know what to do to make sure I'm not having complications. As long as I stay conscious, that is.

Speaking of that, it's time to squirm my way to the edge of my bed again and try to stay awake. I take a deep breath and move through the pain, gritting my teeth, stopping to splint the Mississippi when I need a moment because it hurts too much to go any farther. I force myself to scoot to the side of the mattress and plant my feet on the cold tile. I have a few false starts, because I can't will myself out of fainting, no matter how much I don't want to black out. I have to lie back down for a bit and try again. Finally, I make enough progress without passing out, and I sit a few minutes, panting a little, catching my breath, and letting the spots recede. Sometimes a nurse comes in and watches me try to move, her hand resting supportively on my shoulder to spot me. Sometimes, I do it by myself because I'm *going* to get to my babies. I am. I will. I. Can. Do. This. Yow. This hurts.

Once I master sitting up—a skill I used to take for granted—Jason gets a wheelchair and trucks me to the NICU so I can visit our kids again. I finally get to hold one of them more than just in my hands hovering over the mattress, though they do place Spencer onto my lap with the thick foam pad he's lying on. Transferring him on the pad helps keep all of his gear collected without pulling on him, but I can't get a good feel of his little body. At least he's back close to me and can hear my voice whispering to him. I'm sure he knows his mama has got him again. But come to think of it, he might be wondering why no one is currently kicking him.

Pretty soon, I can make at least a couple of trips a day to see them. When Jason is at work, I have to wait for a nurse to come get me. I guess I need to mend my relationship with the Pink Ladies. I bet they'd give me a lift.

I need more time than most new moms to recuperate. They are giving me five days to get my act together. Just when I can take the pain without too much medication, and I'm starting to totter along without fainting, I get discharged. I wish they'd give me Cyndi's blood donation. I wonder if I can get it in a container to go....

It is bittersweet to leave the hospital. Of course I want to get out of here and go home after so long. But I don't want to leave without my babies. But since I've known from the start I'd have to do exactly that, I don't waste energy fretting about it. I'm glad I've had these five days to recover with them just down the hall. Most moms get so much less time. Some have to deliver using the drive-through window that hospitals now use because of insurance limits on hospital stays. You drive up, push 'em out, hand 'em over, proceed to the next window, and pay. They hand the kid back through the window, clean and wrapped. While they hand him out, they're on the headset talking to the next lady in line behind you, "Breathe, pant, pussshhhh. Ah, there he is. Your total is $5,000. Please advance to the next window, and have a nice day. Welcome to McBirthing Center. Can I take your vitals?"

The sooner I get home, the sooner I can sleep, and the sooner I can regain my strength so I can come back. It's Monday evening, January 25, and a nurse pushes me in a wheelchair through the main doors of the hospital to meet Jason who has pulled up the car to the front circular driveway. Taking plenty of time and bracing my Mississippi incision with my hands, I shuffle into my seat. We wave goodbye to the nurse and drive away from the hospital. Oh, to see the sky again. Actually, it is dark by the time we leave the hospital, but just knowing it is up there, wide and open, is enough for me. I am free again. We need to drive to a completely different part of town to pick up a rental breast pump before going home, but the drive is exquisite. Seeing houses with yellow lights glowing out their window panes, watching cars on the road with their headlights shining in my eyes, it is amazing what catches my attention and thrills me after nearly two months in the hospital. It's like I've been let out of the clink.

By the time we pick up the pump and arrive back at our quadplex, I nearly fall over. I haven't been upright this long for months. It's a good thing there are only four steps down into our garden apartment. I waddle down and walk into my long lost home. It's *so good* to be back. And to sleep in my own bed. Ah, sweet home, sweet.

CHAPTER 35

THE BIG BIRD TRAGEDY

We've all had those days when we've gotten too close to that proverbial edge of going absolutely certifiable bonkers. They come more frequently, I think, when you're parenting young children. Universally, every single little kid has some innate ability to make grown, previously well-adjusted adults lose their grip on reality, forsake all learned coping mechanisms, and act completely bring-on-the-straitjacket nuts.

Guess what. When you put four of them together, all the same age, day after day after day, you can get to that breaking point even faster than you usually would.

At three, my kids were totally into the Sesame Street scene. Each child had his or her favorite character, each one's preference reflecting the color assignment I'd given them when they came home from the hospital to keep track of their bottles first, and then after that their blankets, clothes, toothbrushes, backpacks, and everything else they individually owned. Even now, good friends know who has which color, and not so close friends wonder why their belongings seem to always fall into one color palate. (When they start the inevitable therapy that all people need to work out the damage done to them by their parents, I'm sure they'll need to have some intensive work on their obsessions with certain colors.) We often went to the "Bert and Ernie Store" to see how we could add to their Sesame Street collections. There we found gently used stuffed animals or other Sesame Street toys for them to enjoy. (They called all thrift stores the Bert and Ernie Store for a long time.) One Christmas I sewed almost life-size versions of their favorite characters using ping pong balls for Cookie Monster's eyes and real toddler shoes for Bert and Ernie. Cookie had a giant fur chocolate chip cookie Velcroed onto his hand, Big Bird had his teddy bear, Ernie his rubber ducky, and Bert, a little canister of oatmeal.

Sesame Street was pretty sacred in our family.
Until that day. That day I went too close to the brink.
From the Bert and Ernie Store we'd acquired a very

cute seven-inch Big Bird toy, a windup yellow tricycle with Big Bird peddling it with his enormous orange feet. His legs went 'round and 'round, turning the wheels, moving the trike across the floor. One day, his windup key stopped working, and the coil spring wouldn't tighten up anymore to make him go. As a can-do, Rosie the Riveter kind of handywomen, I took the broken toy into the laundry room to fix while the kids napped. I sat in the middle of the basement concrete floor and started to work on it. Unfortunately, I was having a really hard day, coping with four three-year-olds, looking in the face of being stuck at home *always and forever*, and just all that *stuff* that every parent knows becomes more than one can cope with on certain days. And Big Bird's tricycle breaking down was one too many losses that day. I was working on the spring mechanism, and I couldn't get it to go back in right. It kept slipping. It kept unwinding, just like I was doing. And pretty soon, I couldn't take it anymore. Sadly, I'd brought along the toolbox that included the hammer in it. One doesn't need a hammer to work on a spring-driven mechanism. But my hand reached over to grab the handle, and my mind went with it.

With the first whack, bits of the trike flew to the far walls of the laundry room. And the spring didn't work even a tiny bit better than it had before. With a few more whacks, Big Bird was flying. In several pieces. By then I couldn't stop myself. I beat that toy to smithereens. There was nothing I could do. It just came out of me.

When Big Bird was no more, along with his obliterated cute little tricycle, I sat there in the middle of the laundry room panting, wondering what had just happened—to me, to Big Bird, and to his trike. Some catharsis. Good thing the kids were safely, blissfully sleeping upstairs in their beds. I picked up by hand the orange foot that had landed in the laundry basket and all the other fragments I could find of Big Bird that had flown into the nooks and crannies of the room. Then I got the broom and dust pan and started sweeping the tiny bits too small to recognize. When the pieces were cleaned up and tied into a small garbage bag, I hid it in the trash bin, smoothed my hair, and waited at the kitchen table with a cup of tea for the kids to wake up from their naps. Once they were awake, I'd have to sit down with them and break the news that we didn't have a Big Bird on a tricycle windup toy anymore. If they asked why, I'd have to tell them the truth. Mom went a little too close to the brink, and then the hammer fell on Big Bird. They'd understand.

CHAPTER 36

NOTES ON BEING NICU PARENTS

Because of my C-section, I won't be able to drive for a month—though we don't have a second car anyway, and Jason uses the one we do have to go to work. I need to find a way to get to the hospital during the day when he's at work. There are some people from our church, which we've hardly been to because of all that happened in the previous year, who have offered to pick me up and take me to the hospital in the morning. It's nice to meet some other moms. Terri and Cathy are two of my new friends, each with three kids of their own. Cathy even has twins. After they drop me off, I stay at the hospital as long as I can tolerate being upright, increasing my time there as my stamina improves. I rotate around to each of the kids' Isolettes to hold, bathe, and feed them. Sometimes feeding is simply holding them with binkies in their mouths while the breast milk drains down a tube into their stomachs. The pacifier is so they'll associate the feeling of getting full with sucking on a nipple. I dress them in clothes as much as possible because wearing clothes helps premie babies gain weight. Go figure. It's like when I got dressed when I was on bed rest, I guess. It made me feel and do better. Maybe it also helped *me* gain weight. I sure needed to. Bed rest was making me lose muscle mass, plus I couldn't eat enough for the five of us. By the end of the pregnancy, I'd gained only fifty pounds total. At delivery, I lost twenty-five of that. Twelve and a half of it was pure baby.

I have many premie outfits to dress them in because when we lived in Chicago, I started to develop a business to sell Itsy Bitsy Baby Wear. I never launched it because I had trouble finding snaps that wouldn't get hot under the NICU warmer lights, and I didn't really know how to start a business. But in the meantime, I'd made many sleepers, dresses, tops and bottoms, and overalls for three-pound babies. Now I can put those to good use and keep my babies dressed in matching jammies and itsy bitsy clothes.

After I spend the day in the NICU, one of my new friends comes back mid-afternoon and gives me a return ride home. I rest, and when Jason gets home from work, we go back to the hospital after the 7:00 p.m. change of shift for the evening.

Some nights we get into the NICU late and they've already started feeding the babies without us. We're late because we can't find any parking. Too many employees are using the parking garage and most of the spaces are taken. We drive around and around, waiting and watching for an open spot. I've heard the administration is cracking down on employees and telling them they have to park elsewhere, but we have yet to see the relief. It's very frustrating to have something so banal as parking prevent us from being able to care for our babies ourselves. I hope this will be resolved soon. After the car window was broken out, and with my stamina not completely recovered yet, we don't want to park blocks away.

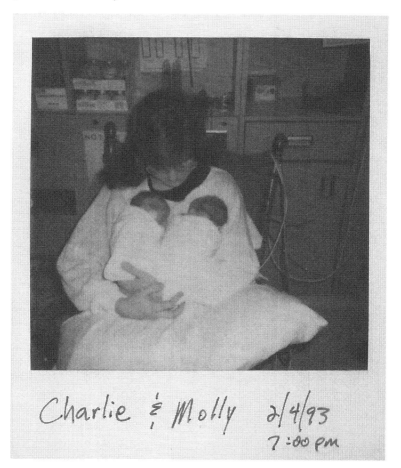

Charlie & Molly 2/4/93
7:00 pm

The babies' overall progress is great. They're all done with the blue bili lights, with Charlie having had the hardest time with jaundice and keeping his bilirubin down—a problem common for premies, especially at our high altitude. Their supplemental oxygen requirements are dropping, and they've moved from CPAP to nasal cannulas. All four have gotten breast milk at least through feeding tubes, and some are beginning to learn to nurse or drink from a bottle.

I continue to pump for breast milk constantly. And I mean constantly. The pump has basically become my new appendage. After I nurse Molly or Charlie at the hospital—the two who are improving the fastest—I express more in the hospital breastfeeding room, then go home and pump more. When I initially turn on the machine, the first few cycles of the suction are excruciating, and the experts I consult tell me that's not normal, and I must have an infection. There is absolutely no sign of any infection or any other issue. My belief? It's simply from strapping two Shop-Vacs onto two of the most sensitive parts of my body several times a day. That's bound to cause some discomfort. But I use the meds they insist is the answer (with no change whatsoever), and I keep at it. I want so badly to make this breastfeeding thing work, I'm willing to endure a lot. Of my entire childbearing experience, the only thing I had preconceived expectations about was breastfeeding. I haven't even assumed I would have one baby, let alone four, when all is said and done. But by golly, I am going to breastfeed whoever I do have. So I religiously pump, even when the pain lifts me off the chair each time I flip on the switch.

I don't know if it is because my babies were whisked away from me the second they were born, or that they didn't come home from the hospital with me, or that I had a breast lump removed five years ago, but I tell you, my milk production is not something to be proud of.

When I take my little baggies of watery flaxen milk to the NICU refrigerator to store until my babies can have them, I'm discouraged to set them on the shelf next to the jugs of milk other ladies with one baby have lugged in. Some of them, I swear, roll in kegs of the liquid gold on dollies. I soothe the feelings of my inadequacy by telling myself maybe they can produce a lot more milk than I can, but I produced four times as many babies at once than they did.

We take our victories where we can. Being petty can sometimes bring comfort.

I'll allow myself a moment of juvenile ill will, then I'll stop it and be happy for them. There. I'm done with my pity party. Good for you. Yay. Got milk? You've got plenty. Drink up, kids.

If you're wondering how one goes about nursing four babies at once, you're not alone. When I was newly pregnant (during the three-week window when I was up among the walking), Jason and I were having dinner with my parents who had over an old friend of theirs from out of town whom I hadn't seen in about twenty years. When he heard I was pregnant with four, he—of course, like everyone—had many questions, and having known me as a scrawny pre-teenager, he wasn't the least bit intimidated about asking me all kinds of personal questions. Breastfeeding was one of the topics that fascinated him. Incredulous, he asked if I intended to nurse. I tried not to hide under the table as he ogled my breasts. I steeled myself, sat up straight, and boldly answered that I indeed did plan to. He laughed mockingly, jabbing his index finger toward each of my breasts, and said, "How you gonna do that? You've only got two of those."

I haven't let his skepticism deter me. If there is a way to nurse all four, I'm going to find it.

On echocardiogram, they've found that Molly has three holes in her heart—VSDs, defects in the septum separating her two ventricles. This is a problem because it allows unoxygenated blood from the right side of her heart to cross over and mix with the blood in the left chamber going out to her body, blood which is supposed to be completely saturated with oxygen. As long as she gets supplemental oxygen, she seems to be tolerating the compromised system so far. We'll have to have more echocardiograms in the future to keep tabs on her status and determine if and when she'll need open heart surgery to patch the defects.

Pierce and Spencer are having issues too. They both have PDAs, which is an acronym for a long Latin phrase that means their fetal circulation is still open, which means their blood is bypassing their lungs. When they were inside of me this was a good thing because they weren't using their lungs to breathe air, and my lungs did the respiratory work for all five of us. But now, it's a problem. They need their blood to stop shunting past their lungs. Doing so is sending unoxygenated blood through their little bodies. This increases their dependency on oxygen, plus keeps them from advancing in every area.

There is a medication they can receive up to three times that changes the pressure in their lungs and closes down the fetal circulation. If it doesn't close after three dosages, they'll need to have heart surgery and have a band clamped around the errant vessel to close it.

Pierce ἐ Spencer 2/4/93
7:00 pm

They both receive their first dose. Nothing. They get a second hit. Still no improvement. Okay, so they have one more. And behold, Pierce's PDA closes. Phew. His oxygen levels go right up. But Spencer's does not. He's going to need surgery. But then, without telling me and against typical protocol, for some reason they give him a fourth dose. And what do you know? It works! He doesn't have to go to the OR after all. I am so relieved.

Though Spencer avoids surgery for his heart, it looks like he might need plastic surgery on his arm. The staff didn't keep a close enough eye on his IV site, and the protein they pump in to nourish him until he is on regular milk feedings leaked into the tissue around his IV and burned him. His arm is about as big around as Jason's finger, and now he has a dark hole in his forearm almost as big as a dime. A plastic surgeon is scheduled to evaluate him to determine if he needs a skin graph. I can't believe they let this happen. Everyone *knows* you always keep the insertion site of an IV catheter, plus where it ends beneath the skin, visible so you can confirm the fluid is actually going into the vessel. Because he's such a hard venous stick, they had way too much tape and gauze over his arm hoping to secure it, and for twelve hours they couldn't see that the terrible, caustic fluid was infiltrating into his tissue. It kills me to see how hurt his tiny precious arm is.

July 14, 1998. Road trip ready! Packed and ready to board our "new" 1988 Plymouth Grand Voyager, christened Mini-Van-Gogh by the family. Missionaries going overseas sold it to us for $2500. We were incredibly excited to have a new van, and one fully loaded! (Left to right: Molly, Charlie, Pierce, and Spencer.)

CHAPTER 37

THE RED DUFFLE BAG

When the kids were five, we took our annual summer road trip to Minnesota. The discounts on the train weren't offered anymore, so we used the car. Before leaving, I wrote everything down we'd need, gathered supplies, checked items off lists, and packed an incredible amount of gear to get through a week at the farm. For the kids, I used a huge red duffel bag, designed and made by Jason's cousin who had a cottage industry producing outdoor and camping accessories. The duffle bag included an identical cosmetic bag, a tiny replica of the large one, in which I packed some of my own things. The oversized duffel was perfect for a week's worth of clothes for kids exploring and playing around a farm.

Though we usually drove straight through to save time and money, this trip we splurged and stayed in a motel halfway to Minnesota—somewhere in the middle of

Kansas—so we didn't have to do the entire sixteen-hour drive in one stretch. The break was especially helpful since we'd had a late start, leaving after Jason got off work. When we pulled into the Super 8 parking lot at midnight, it was such a relief to know we'd get some much needed shuteye. The kids were exhausted and tilting sideways in their seats. I felt like tilting myself. But I had work to do first to get the kids to bed.

The motel allowed only up to three kids in a room, but since we couldn't afford an extra room, and since the kids were a set and could really count as only one, and since it was the most stupid rule I'd heard in a long time, we just hoped no one was counting, or they'd think they kept seeing the same kid over and over.

Our room was on an upstairs floor of the motel, so we both hitched up a sleeping kid in each arm and hiked up the staircase. (Did you know that sleeping children weigh twice as much as conscious children?) As the four lethargic, semi-conscious kids lay crosswise on one of the two beds, I began pulling off shoes and socks. Jason unloaded the car, bringing up the luggage. He asked what I specifically needed so he wouldn't have to completely empty the car.

For the kids I said, "I just need the red duffel bag."

When he came back and started locking up the motel room door, I said, "Where's the red duffel bag?"

He said, "Right there," pointing to it on the other bed. He was pointing at the miniature red duffel cosmetic bag.

"No, I need the big one."

He went back down to look some more. When he came back, he could only shrug. "That's the only red duffel bag."

"Didn't you load the red duffel bag? It was on the bed. I said to be sure to bring the red duffel bag."

I was a little frustrated.

"I thought you meant that one." The little one.

The big red duffel had everything in it. Not only clothes, but toothbrushes, underwear, *everything*.

I took a deep, loud breath. A noisy sigh. An "I-can't-believe-you-did-that-can-you-hear-the-subtext-in-this-sigh-that's-intentionally-loud-enough-to-make-sure-you-know-how-frustrated-I-am-right-now" sigh.

Using most of Jason's week's supply of undershirts, we dressed the kids for bed, getting them out of their [now only] play clothes. Maybe he thought I was being quiet not to rouse the children. I think I was probably doing some kind of passive-aggressive silent treatment to make sure he knew he'd blown it. In silence, I used my toothbrush to brush all their teeth, and we got them to bed. They were so droopy and nearly asleep that they didn't notice we weren't using their own Ernie or Bert or Big Bird or Oscar toothbrushes.

By morning, I was a little less of a grumpy pants, having gotten about four hours of sleep, so we made a plan. We'd stop somewhere along the way and find a store to see if we could buy some clothes. And underwear. And toothbrushes. And everything you need for an entire week on the farm with four kids.

At a Wal-Mart in Des Moines, we hit pay dirt. A rack of Garanimals clothing was on clearance. Garanimals are those clothes that are interchangeable stretchy polyester. They're easy for kids to put on themselves and made to match no matter what combo a kid will come up with. But even though they were on clearance, I couldn't bring myself to buy a new summer wardrobe in their current sizes so far into the season. They'd outgrow them before they could use them again. So I went up a size for each. Plenty of room to grow. And move. And to lose their pants running across the farmyard if they weren't careful. But what a bargain.

We got new toothbrushes and underwear too, then got back on the road and headed to the farm with only an hour or so lost.

We had a great visit at the farm. We went boating with Jason's cousin Tom. We had a Christmas-in-July celebration with all four families exchanging gifts. And we had an early party for Jack's seventieth birthday coming in August.

The house had a lot more of the sheetrock covered, some more flooring down, and even had a railing installed where the third story balcony looked out over the living room below. When it was time to go home, no one wanted to say goodbye. Jack—PaJack to our kids—hugged each of the kids and me goodbye, then shook Jason's hand, slipping an envelope of cash into Jason's other hand as they shared their farewells. Jack took care of the cost of the trip, plus the unexpected purchase of the new wardrobes.

Just so you know, when we got home after a week away—tired, sun-soaked, mosquito bitten, and all around vacationed up—we found the big red duffel sitting right there on the bed, full of clothes that were clean, folded, and waiting to be unpacked and put away. See? Not so bad.

CHAPTER 38

NOTES ON BEING DISCHARGED

Molly is scheduled to come home. We have to meet with the home health services rep to go over the oxygen tank and the heart and lung monitor to learn how to use them. It's Sunday, February 21, exactly a month since their birth. We started mid-afternoon, and the whole thing is taking way too long. By the time we finish with the demo and the rep is confident we can use the tank, regulator, and monitor, Molly is exhausted. She's been required to attend the meeting in order for the rep to use the equipment on her for demonstration purposes. Normally, she'd be asleep during this time period because it is between her 1:00 and

4:00 p.m. feedings, because that's what babies do, especially premie babies who are still a month before their due date.

After I tuck Molly back into her bassinette, I tell her nurse—a woman I have never seen in the NICU before—that Molly is exhausted, that her schedule is messed up and not to even try to give her the 4:00 p.m. feeding because no way is she going to eat well, and I'll be back to the hospital to nurse her at 7:00 p.m.

After a nap to rest up before an evening at the hospital, Jason and I are getting ready to leave our apartment for the hospital around 6:30 p.m. when we get a call from the NICU. Something has happened to Molly. She wouldn't eat, and her crazy nurse thought her belly had "blown up" (a thing you watch for in premies because their intestines can get sick if you put milk in them too soon), and she is back in critical condition.

We race to the hospital. When we get there, Molly is no longer in her clothes or bundled in her bassinette like a normal baby who is going home tomorrow. Instead, she is flat out on her back in an open warming bed (the type critical babies lie in), limp as a rag doll, with tubes all over the place, and bruises and blood. She is a mess.

During the past thirty-two days, eleven hours and thirty-three minutes that my kids have lived in the NICU, they've all won the "Can't Get A Line in Me to Save the World" award every single day. They are the hardest IV sticks in a thousand mile radius, and even the best of the NICU nurses, the kind who could place an IV line even in a turnip, *those* nurses have had trouble getting any lines in my kids. So when we walk in and find Molly tortured and incapacitated in only her diaper, laid out like she is near death, some people have been sticking her with needles for the last two hours. Molly has been screaming for *two hours*. Molly, who hours earlier was a healthy, happy, regular baby on her way home without complications, has been starved (now she's missed two feedings) and tortured and totally persecuted for *two hours*. No wonder she looks like death. The idiot who was assigned as her nurse (guess I have some forgiveness issues here I need to work on), the idiot I *told* to leave Molly alone, decided to wake her up at 4:00 p.m., about an hour after we left, and attempted to feed her a bottle. Molly didn't go for it.

Didn't I *say* she wouldn't go for it?

So this woman took it upon herself to diagnose my baby with some kind of bowel blockage, or NEC (necrotizing enterocolitis—if you don't know, you don't want to know—a nasty condition where the bowel dies a bad death). She telephoned an on-call doctor covering for our pediatrician *without even checking with the charge nurse first*. Folks, for anyone not familiar with the way things go down in hospital units, if you're a visiting nurse and you run into trouble, you *do not skip talking to your charge nurse first*. You just don't. No matter how slick a care provider you think you are. You. Just. Don't. So this chick told a doctor who'd never seen my kids and knew nothing about the situation that Molly wasn't eating well. (Did anyone notice I said this would happen? Did I not *tell her* this would happen?) She told the doctor that she thought Molly's belly looked distended. Molly, our little bundle of cuteness who had the most darling little round tummy *all the time*. The idiot doctor gave the stupid nurse orders like this: stop her feedings, start a line, get cultures, get blood gases, poke her all to hell and back, and see what happens.

Besides new punctures and bruises all over her arms and legs, they've also stuck her in the head all over the place trying to get a line in. Now, Molly—who'd had the least need for IVs of the four because of her stellar progress—is as much a pin cushion as her three brothers put together and she has patches of her soft, red hair shaved off in multiple spots. The hair of course will grow back and is something of minimal concern when you're looking at crucial medical intervention, but when you know it is unnecessary, it's adding insult to injury. She could have kept that little semblance of normalcy.

Once they finally got some blood out of her, they ran numerous tests, including setting up cultures to see if she is septic. Of course, I *know* she isn't. I'm not worried about that once I learn what has really happened, that that nurse chick had tried to do what I warned her not to do. (What does concern me is how am I going to get back at this nurse who has hurt my baby. Will I make it quick and painless, or will I draw it out and make it a slow, painful end?)

Molly's discharge is cancelled, and she is kept on "critical" status. It feels like we've slipped back into some nightmare, losing ground and hope.

Once cultures for sepsis are started, the tests have to grow for forty-eight hours and be negative before Molly can be discharged, even though we all know (except for her dumb nurse and that moron on-call doctor) it is a bunch of hooey. Annoying hospital policy to prove that there are no nasty bugs growing in the blood of the victim.

Seeing Molly's poor little self, post-torture, listless and exhausted, is heartbreaking. Not only is it a terrible thing to see her suffer so needlessly, but the whole episode is a bit of a psychological crisis for me. After infertility and miscarriage, where I got to the point of believing I would never have my own baby, then a high-risk pregnancy, where I had no confidence the results would include living children, to the day when I thought "tomorrow I'm taking home my baby," to having that snatched away from me, my brain doesn't know what to do with it all. Coping mechanisms tell me it isn't real, that I am not truly a mom, that I don't really have children, that I am never taking any babies home, that we'll never have children. Weird, yeah? I need therapy. But I have no time for therapy. I must push these disturbing perceptions out of my mind for future counseling sessions, if I can ever work them in, and face the coming hours and days right now.

When our pediatrician comes back on duty after the weekend and finds out what has happened, he is furious. He calls the other doctor who'd covered for him and reams him out right there at the nurses' station. A friend of mine who works in the NICU overhears the conversation. When our pediatrician gets off the phone, he asks my eavesdropping friend who the incompetent nurse was because he intends to ream her out too. (My friend, who is becoming a better friend every minute, is unprofessional enough to do me the satisfying favor of relaying the entire episode to me blow-by-blow.) She tells me she answered the pediatrician defiantly, "Nuh-uh. She's *mine*." As in mafia style, I'm taking care of that woman myself.

(Nothing is in the newspaper about it, so I don't know.)

By Wednesday Molly is back on her feedings. All of her lab work has cleared. Her bruised arms, legs, and scalp are scabbed up and starting to heal from the unexpected *unnecessary* needle pokes. She can wear clothes again. I bundle her up to take her home, to break her out of that place—though it will never be far from my thoughts because I have to leave my three other babies there.

Jason is at work, but I don't want to wait a minute longer than I have to. Though good people have taken great care of me and my kids, I hold on for the day somewhere out there in the future when we will take home *all* of our babies and never have to come here again. So I kiss the boys farewell for another of too many times, vowing their day is coming. Driving with my dad in his car, I take Molly home, celebrating that we've made a huge step in the right direction. Maybe I really am a mom after all.

Once Jason gets home, my parents come back over to our apartment and take care of Molly while we return to the hospital to see the boys for the evening. Pierce was supposed to come home within a day or two of Molly, with the others to follow soon after that. But he's having feeding problems again. And Spencer's having trouble too, for that matter. It's like they'll crawl a couple of steps forward but then one backward. Neither can get past a certain point with feedings. Their bellies swell up and the milk has to be stopped and drainage tubes put back in. Their oxygen needs stay in flux too.

The neonatologist thinks there isn't sufficient oxygen perfusion to their organs, and it's most apparent in their guts and lungs. After having blood drawn for all of their lab tests over the many days since birth, they've been depleted. It doesn't take many vials of blood taken for lab work to drain too much of their blood volume. They only have about half a cup of blood in their tiny bodies. Their doctor wants to give them each a blood transfusion.

Man, I really don't want this to happen. I voice my worry about the possible complications of them receiving blood, but the staff assures me it's well-screened and safe. Of course, I know this. I've given babies more transfusions than I can count. I know how it works. But still. These are my babies.

Jason reports to the blood bank to get screened himself to see if they can use his blood which is O-negative, the universal donor type anyone can receive, but they say it will take too long to process for Spencer and Pierce to get it soon enough. So we go ahead and give consent, but I'm on edge until the transfusions are over and they've had no negative reaction or complications.

And the blood is like magic. Suddenly, they can eat, digest, poo—everything works like it should. Funny how all our parts like blood. Kind of essential, so it seems. They have a complete turn around, and it looks like they'll be following Molly home any day now.

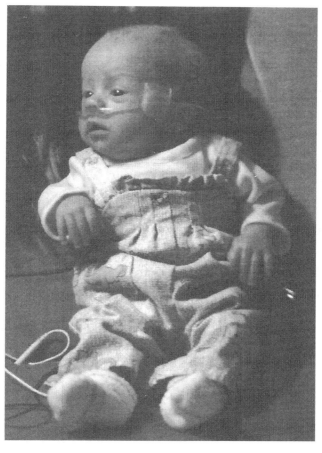

Molly's first day home at four pounds, nine-and-a-half ounces

PaJack reading on the floor with his grandkids, April 1996

CHAPTER 39

THE REMEMBERING

Jack passed away. Three weeks shy of his eighty-fourth birthday he had a sudden illness. It was the end of July, a month before our kids would start their sophomore year of college. After an urgent phone call from his stepmom, Jason boarded a plane to the Minneapolis-Saint Paul airport, then sped in a rental car to Mayo Clinic in Rochester. He reached Jack's bedside a few hours before he had to say goodbye. The kids and I followed in the van. Charlie took the wheel so I wouldn't have to and drove us the entire way himself.

After spending the night in a motel in Kansas, we arrived the next day at the big house on the farm as Jason's siblings' families gathered there with us. A lot of time and experiences had passed since Jason and I lived in those two basement rooms of that unfinished house. In 2012, some of the trim still wasn't on and some of the floors were still bare and the windows undressed. But my relationship with Jack had become good. We got along well, felt respect and love for each other, and we laughed a lot whenever we were together. He took care of us all generously. He was already missed.

Before we arrived at the farm to reunite our immediate family, it was anguishing to be separated from Jason during such a difficult time. I was so distracted and worried that when we packed up the van and readied to head east, I forgot to turn off the garden hose. I was out watering a few outdoor plants moments before our departure, hoping the tomato and squash plants and the peach trees would tolerate the summer heat while we were gone. Then I set down the hose and walked away and got in the car. I didn't know I'd done it until several days later when my sister called. She'd found a notice from the utility company posted on our front door that we should check for a water leak because they'd detected a spike in our water usage. My sister found the hose flowing in the back yard, right where I'd dropped it. (The bill was nearly $600.)

After Jack's funeral, we returned home to Colorado. Jason came with us in the car instead of using his return plane ticket. The credit with the airline provided Jason and me the opportunity to visit Chicago two months later for our twenty-fifth wedding anniversary. We'd not been back to Chicago since the day we took apart Carl's doorjamb and drove out of town with a truck loaded by the skinniest movers you'd ever seen.

On the day of our anniversary, we returned to Fourth Presbyterian Church and stood in the aisle of the breathtaking sanctuary where we'd exchanged our vows a quarter of a century before. Then we went across the street to the Hancock Building and had lunch at the Signature Room, an exquisite restaurant on the ninety-fifth floor. We ate at a window table, gazing out over Chicago and Lake Michigan, where we'd met by the brownies on that boat and didn't even know it.

On the trip we visited and dined with friends who'd been at our wedding, who had worked alongside us, and who had played with us around Chicagoland. We went to our former places of work to see how the sites had changed. They'd universally developed much tighter security, for one thing, and some had new structures (and even different addresses). We rode the bus and El to all our old apartment buildings. Serendipitously, we found at our old Lincoln Park high-rise one of our old (former *and* elderly, now) doormen who still worked there. Ransom caught us up on the changes with the building, which had converted from apartments to condos, plus he updated us on the other doormen we used to know and see every day. One had passed away, and another still worked there, though it was his day off. We walked around the city and its hidden wonders like we used to do. One delightful encounter came when we visited the Newberry Library where an especially amiable librarian took us to the secret staff staircase "cage" featured in *The Time Traveler's Wife*, one of my all-time favorite books. It's where the protagonist always feared he would reappear and be trapped.

It was an unforgettable and unparalleled trip, to return to where it all started for us. Little did we know back then what life had in store for us, when we first met, married, and then dared to hope we might someday have a baby.

CHAPTER 40

NOTES ON BEING REUNITED

The plastic surgeon evaluated Spencer and determined he won't have a skin graph. They're treating the wound on his arm with burn protocol (it's a chemical burn), changing the sterile dressing frequently with special burn ointment. He's going to have a thick scar, but at least he won't have the additional donor site wound that would have come with harvesting a skin graph.

And though Spencer and Pierce have improved rapidly after their transfusions, Charlie has moved to the front of the line, and the doctor is discharging him home. Once again Jason is working, so I need to borrow my dad's car to have transportation. He comes with me, and since Molly isn't old enough yet to stay home alone, and my mom works during the day, we bring Molly with us to fetch her little brother.

Every time we arrive at the NICU, we have to go through the procedure of "scrubbing in" to wash away the nasty doorknob germs we might be carrying in with us. After we're squeaky clean, we don long gowns to cover our street clothes. There is a little area by the sinks for us parents where we can put our belongings, with wall hooks for our coats and bags.

3/1 Charlie's going home

I drove today and carry the car keys. My dad is carrying Molly in her car seat. As I hang my coat on the hook so I can scrub in, an inner voice tells me to put the car keys into my pants pocket instead of leaving them in my coat where I normally would—with my gloves, a few loose dollars, and a Kleenex. Hmm. A little odd, but okay. I slip the keys into my pants pocket and put it out of my mind. Then I scrub in, enter the NICU, and go on to do what is necessary to break out Charlie. We pause for a nurse to take a picture.

Once the necessary paperwork is signed, and we visit with my two babies who are still doing time, we gather the pair that are officially mine again and head for the door.

But my coat isn't there.

It isn't anywhere.

With some investigation, we find out the parent area has been targeted lately by an unknown band of coat thieves, to which my coat has apparently fallen victim. I hope that Kleenex in my pocket was well-used and icky. How dare they? Parents here are grieving, yearning, sorrowful, in pain—and some person of low character is stalking their coat rack. Not to mention that hospital security knew about this but failed to inform us of the risk we've been taking by trusting our belongings to their inviting, benign-looking coat hooks.

Frankly, I don't know why that inner voice told me to take the car keys with me but neglected to say, "Take your coat with you too, with your favorite *genuine leather* gloves in the pockets that you got in Chicago when you used to have money, and the pocket change that will take Jason a half day of work to replace, and keep it with you at all times." But at least I have my dad's car keys, and we can go home.

But I'm really irritated about my coat. I got that London Fog jacket for our honeymoon in England. We don't have the money to replace it, or the leather gloves.

My only other pair are old thin knit gloves with a hole in one finger. But maybe the thief is poorer than we are. Maybe they really need a nice coat. I should let it go. But maybe they just did it for a prank and threw it in a garbage bin for a good laugh.

I'll probably never know. I must let it go. Forgive the crook and move on. Quit scanning every crowd I see, looking at everyone walking the halls of the hospital, searching for my green coat. It's going to drive me crazy. But I have other things to worry about. And even bigger things to be thankful for.

Molly, Charlie, and I have four days to settle into a routine. They love being back together again and seem to find comfort in each other's presence. I nurse them both, usually at the same time, then pump afterwards to keep my milk production up as much as possible. It's busy but very peaceful. And it's so good to have them home!

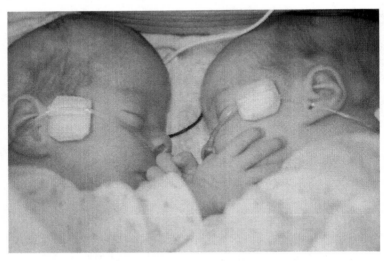

I go back to the hospital every time I can, which depends on finding someone to stay with Molly and Charlie at home while I go. I'm so very, very eager to get them all home. It's simply wretched to have half home and half still in the hospital.

On Thursday, March 4, we get the go-ahead to bring home both Pierce and Spencer. Our NICU nurse friend comes over to our apartment after work and takes care of Molly and Charlie so Jason and I can go to the hospital and pick up our other two children. We don't even wait for the hospital newborn photographer to take the routine discharge photos. We just want to get our babies and get the heck out of there. We sign on the dotted lines as quickly as possible. And finally, as the sun is setting on this long-awaited day, we take home the rest of our litter.

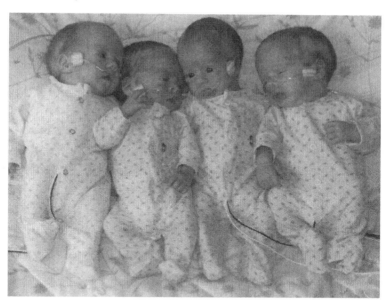

CHAPTER 41

THE GRATITUDE

The days that followed were happy but hard. Jason had to go to work that next day when all four kids were home for the first time, so it was just the five of us together. That early in their homecoming and because it was so sweet to finally have my babies to myself, I wouldn't have wanted an outsider there (not yet anyway), but it was a tough challenge to meet everyone's needs on my own. The day was crazy trying to get them all fed, comforted when they fussed, and tucked in to sleep at least a little before the next feeding. I knew it was probably nuts for me to want to breastfeed all of them, but I was going to give it my absolute best shot. I was determined to prove myself to people like my parents' old friend who'd mockingly asked back when I was only nine weeks pregnant, "How you gonna do that? You've only got two of those."

I had a system. I'd been practicing with Charlie and Molly for the few days we had before the other two came home. My plan was to nurse two at the same time, then give bottles to the other two, then rotate for the next feeding. Unfortunately, since I was the only one home that first day, some babies had to wait to get their bottles. Spencer and Pierce were new on the scene and didn't understand the routine yet. They thought once the dinner bell rang, everyone got to step up to the chow line to dig in. They were unaware kids usually didn't come in litters, and that there would have to be some give and take. After a few feedings, I figured out how to use pillows to hold two babies breastfeeding while also propping a baby or two next to me on pillows to feed them bottles at the same time. But I really needed Jason home to help with that set up, so the first day, it was two at a time at best. And being only six weeks old, the ones who had to wait weren't very patient.

On the first feeding after Jason left for work, I spent almost four hours getting everyone fed. Once the last baby was finished eating, it was basically time to start feedings all over again, but we were all exhausted and needed sleep more than anything. I put them in their cribs, and they went to sleep. Phew.

Then I realized the homecare nurse was supposed to come over any minute to visit and see how we were getting along. The doorbell heralding her arrival would annihilate the tranquility I'd worked so hard to achieve. Even if Publishers Clearing House showed up at my door with one of their giant checks and rang the bell, I would have no other choice but to shoot them. I grabbed the phone and paged the visiting nurse. I waited, worrying I hadn't called her in time. She'd been over once before, after Charlie got home, and the only reason I agreed to even accept the service was that I thought some of the visits would replace our trips to the pediatrician for weight checks. I had done home nursing visits on new babies myself, and I didn't need anyone to check their belly buttons for me or tell me how many wet diapers they needed in a day. When she called back, I explained I had just gotten all of them to sleep after a horrendous morning. She could come over and sit and stare at me, maybe even have tea, but she wasn't touching any baby of mine. Boy, was she ticked. And then I found out the pediatrician wanted to see them in the office just as often anyway, whether or not they were weighed by a homecare nurse. That settled it for me. I cancelled the whole service.

We somehow survived the rest of the day until Jason got home from work. But I was pretty worn out.

That weekend, I finally put my shirt back on and decided the breastfeeding thing was for the birds. At least for all four of them. Molly always nursed easily, so she won the prize. Except for an occasional turn for Charlie, the whole canteen was hers, both taps for the asking. The boys were out of the running. They'd have to brown-bag it. The freezer held all the little bags of milk I'd worked so diligently to store up while they were in the hospital, so the boys would get their breast milk. It would just have to be delivered by a bottle. That stash lasted, oh, about six hours. Then it was on to the baby formula.

They all were on oxygen and cardiac monitors, filling our little apartment to the brim with equipment. A wall was lined with four four-foot tall oxygen tanks, and each baby was attached to their tank by fifty feet of oxygen tubing, which was tangled into a hopeless mess by the end of each day. The monitors seldom alarmed for true bradycardia (a drop in heart rate), but they frequently screamed their ice-pick-in-the-ear alarm if a wire came loose or twisted—usually in the middle of the night.

The week after they came home, we activated the "Quad Squad." A crew of twenty-five to thirty volunteers, mostly church friends of my parents, began coming over to help. They worked for four-hour shifts, starting at seven in the morning and staying until seven in the evening. Other kind, generous, blessed souls took turns bringing us meals.

One day during my pregnancy, Cyndi had mentioned something about her leave of absence from her job when the kids were born.

I looked at her, confused. "Leave of absence? What are you talking about?"

"I'm taking a month off to help."

"Really?" I asked, astonished.

"Of course," she said, like it was ordained in the stars and everyone knew it.

Three days after the kids came home, Cyndi was at our door at 10:30 p.m. Every Sunday to Thursday night for four weeks she sat in our living room, staying awake all night, holding down the fort so we could sleep. When a second baby awoke, I joined her, letting Jason sleep so he'd be able to keep his eyes open at work the next day.

Sleep was a huge issue. For so long, I was so sleep deprived, I couldn't see straight. When I took all four into their first follow-up appointment with their doctor, I stood in the exam room and cried. Nothing had happened. I just cried.

Our pediatrician said, "Well, you're the one who wanted them all home," like I could have or would have left some at the hospital indefinitely.

I said through my emotional sniffling, "Of course I wanted them home. I'm just so tired."

Now, much of those first days, months, years, are a blur to me. Without my journals; my Day-Timer with my quick notes, thoughts, and happenings scribbled in the boxes; my letters to friends they kindly sent back to me at my request; and my boxes upon boxes of photos and shelves of VHS tapes to remind me of our journey, I wouldn't be able to tell my story. When I think back over the past many years, my most common thought is how grateful I am. Though I often just got through what I had to do, not paying much attention in the beginning to any supernatural help or companionship I was getting, now in hindsight I can so clearly see the ways we've been taken care of, the mercies we've received, the provisions that have come. When I am down, overwhelmed, having a pity party, or wondering how I'm going to get through the next challenge—which some days is just getting up and facing a new day—I intentionally and specifically count our blessings, and I say a word of thanks. I say thank you that I met Jason, and he's been my partner in this crazy adventure and has walked every single step by my side. I say thank you that my babies weren't born that night when all hope seemed to be lost. I say thank you that every one of my babies was healthy and had no damage at birth. That Molly's VSDs closed spontaneously and she didn't need open heart surgery. That when the doctor thought Pierce had cerebral palsy, and when Spencer stopped breathing and turned blue and I couldn't get him to start again, and later when Charlie's hand was crushed in a fire door, and when Jason had his bicycle accident, everyone came through okay. That even on days when I didn't think I'd make it through, I did. I'm thankful that my kids are grown up now and are fantastic human beings who text me and call me and talk to me and hug me and love me. I'm grateful that on that day so long ago in the doctor's office I heard a whisper into my soul that no matter what happened, every step of the way, we would not be alone—and I'm thankful that it was absolutely true.

COLOR PHOTOS

Thank you so much for reading this paperback version of *Babies by the Litter*. If you're like me, you love holding a book in your hands to read far more than using an electronic reader. Though one drawback of a physical book is the publishing costs, which often limit the use of color in the printing. The good news is, I've uploaded all the photos, plus some extras for fun, on my website. Simply visit the special page I've created for you real book readers and enjoy the full color photography I've been taking (or collecting, for the pictures taken of me) for three decades. The address is cherigillard.com/photos.

ABOUT THE AUTHOR

Cheri Gillard started her adult life as a registered nurse. Once her quadruplets came along, she continued the writing she started while still in nursing. Her first piece was an article in 1991 for Procter & Gamble on helpful feeding techniques for hospitalized babies who tend to throw up on you. After writing books, curricula, and working as an editor for several Christian publishing houses over many years, she expanded into fiction and has five novels available for your reading pleasure. After blogging every day for a year, which only lasted eight months in reality because her health is a constant challenge and got in the way of that goal, she now blogs weekly plus frequently posts photos and videos of the babies on Instagram with fun anecdotes about raising quadruplets—a pace that gets along much better with her stupid myalgic encephalomyelitis and fibromyalgia. She and her superhero husband live in Colorado.

ACKNOWLEDGMENTS

Thank you, Pierce, for reading, editing, critiquing, suggesting—even when you were on your way out of town for the summer. I appreciate your insight and feedback, as well as encouragement. How fun to have you grow up from the little guy forgotten in the car reading to an expert who can help make my vision come to fruition. You know you're my favorite.

Thank you, Spencer, for designing, consulting, and making recommendations so that my memoir could be far better than I'd ever dreamed, with every detail coordinated and margins and fonts designed in ways I didn't know were possible. Even after exhausting, full days at work doing graphic design, when I sent you my SOSes, you responded like I'd activated the bat signal and you rescued me. Thanks, too, for getting me squared away on Instagram. You know you're my favorite.

And for searching basement bins or top shelves for shoeboxes storing my old letters and returning them to me (and keeping them in the first place!), I am grateful to Pat Hettwer, Jeanne Hoppe, Kathy Jarvi, Peggy Johnson, and my mom, Janell. Cyndee Larson, I so appreciate your meticulous work to help make sure I dotted my i's and crossed my t's.

CONNECT WITH THE AUTHOR

In addition to this non-fiction memoir, I have several fiction titles available, including a highly-praised and award-winning time travel trilogy, *The Nephilim Redemption Series*. If you'd prefer a suspense thriller over paranormal stories, try giving my medical thriller, *The Clone's Mother*, a read. You can see all my titles on my website, cherigillard.com. While you're there, you can also sign up to receive my blog or connect with me with any questions or comments you may have. Follow me on Instagram (cheri_and_quads) or my Facebook page (cheri.gillard.writer), to see lots of fun stories and quadruplet photos. And as we all know, online reviews are the key to spreading the word about books we like; if you would kindly leave a review for *Babies by the Litter* at your favorite review spots, I'd be forever grateful, and we could count ourselves the best of friends.

18294814R00214

Made in the USA
San Bernardino, CA
20 December 2018